BANNED BOOKS FOR KIDS

Reading Lists and Activities for Teaching Kids to Read Censored Literature

PAT R. SCALES

ALAAmericanLibraryAssociation

sourcebooks

Copyright © 2023 by the American Library Association
Cover and internal design © 2023 by Sourcebooks
Cover design by Sourcebooks
Cover images © YuliaShlyahova/Adobe Stock
Internal design by Tara Jaggers/Sourcebooks

Sourcebooks and the colophon are registered trademarks of Sourcebooks.

Published by Sourcebooks
P.O. Box 4410, Naperville, Illinois 60567-4410
(630) 961-3900
sourcebooks.com

Cataloging-in-Publication Data is on file with the Library of Congress.

Printed and bound in the United States of America.
VP 10 9 8 7 6 5 4 3 2 1

For

Barbara and John Sanders

for loaning me Sara and Anne Marie,
Ragan, Mary Kate, Danny, and Austin

CONTENTS

FOREWORD

I f we could clone educators, I'd clone Pat Scales and send her to guide, support, and encourage every new school librarian and teacher. But until that's a possibility, I'll just have to spread the word any way I can. For those of you who aren't familiar with her work, I'll begin in the mid-1970s when Pat's students at Greenville Middle School in Greenville, South Carolina, did a telephone interview with me. Their questions were thoughtful, sometimes difficult, and often laced with humor. I got the feeling they listened to my answers as carefully as they had prepared their questions. So I was pleased when Pat and I finally met in person a year or so later at Pat's first American Library Association conference. My editor, Dick Jackson, invited Pat to join his table at the Newbery-Caldecott dinner. I'd never been to a Newbery-Caldecott celebration, either. I still remember what I wore, because I had recently moved to New Mexico and I came decked out in a long, gauzy number, with silver and turquoise around my neck. More importantly, I remember Mildred Taylor's acceptance speech for *Roll of Thunder, Hear My Cry*.

It wasn't easy to talk at that dinner but when I heard about Communicate through Literature, the program Pat had started at Greenville Middle School, I was fascinated. Here was a young school librarian inviting the parents of her students into her library once a month, without the kids, to talk about contemporary young adult books. Her goals were to help them get comfortable with the books their children might be reading and to encourage them to use literature to spark open and honest conversations with their kids. In doing so, Pat helped these parents remember their own adolescent years, bringing back all those feelings they had managed to forget, and eased their fears and concerns about having their kids read books dealing with real life. Before long, in Greenville, parents and kids were sharing books. Pat was right—the characters in these novels made it easier to talk about subjects and feelings that were on the kids' minds, though until now they had never brought them up at home.

In 1981, when I started The Kids Fund, a small foundation whose goal it was to help bring parents and kids together (because by then I was receiving volumes of mail from kids who wished they could talk openly and honestly with their parents), Pat Scales and Communicate through Literature were our first grant recipient. The stipend was small, but somehow the *Today* show got word of it and asked if they could do a story on Pat's program. When Pat agreed, they sent a film crew to Greenville to interview some of her students and their parents.

Pat and I appeared on the show together, live from New York, to talk about her work. What I remember best about our segment (aside from how nervous we were and that Pat was wearing blue) was that after showing clips of parents and kids at home talking about books, Bryant Gumbel came at us as if approaching the enemy. He led off his attack with, "Yeeah...but will it play in Peoria?" His manner and question left me speechless, but Pat's priceless answer, a long, perplexed "Huh...?", said it all.

Undaunted by her experience on the *Today* show, Pat went back to Greenville and continued to do what she does best—teach and communicate. She worked with her students, their parents, and other librarians and teachers. In 1983, she was honored by the American Association of School Librarians with the American Association of

School Librarians/Social Issues Resource Series Intellectual Freedom Award for her Communicate through Literature program.

At a time when fear was starting to creep into both the school library and the classroom, when some school principals were beginning to worry about anything that could be taken as controversial, and you never knew when some zealot might come into your library waving a book and demanding its removal, Pat never had an issue with censorship. Maybe because parents and students alike trusted and respected her, just as she trusted and respected them. Maybe because she could always explain, in a clear and sensible way, why the books in her program were important to her students. And maybe she was just lucky (not all teachers and librarians survived that era). Luck or not, Pat would fight to her last breath to protect the rights of her students. She's helped me and countless others in defending the rights of all young people to be intellectually free. Most recently she's been telling me, with her usual enthusiasm, about teaching the First Amendment to eighth graders and high school students. And I've been yapping, in my usual way, about sharing her methods with other librarians and teachers. So I welcome this book with my own enthusiasm and high hopes. And say, once again, thanks, Pat. Bravo!

JUDY BLUME
Foreword from First Edition
2001

PREFACE

I think I have always been a proponent of the freedom to read; I just didn't know how to articulate it until I was an adult and established in my career. I don't feel that my reading was ever censored at home as a child. My dad was an avid reader, and from my early adolescence, I read most of what he read. There was no young adult literature in those days, so I read John Steinbeck and Erskine Caldwell. Did these books affect me? Yes, for all the right reasons. They made me sensitive to society and the ways others live. I learned about other cultures by reading books like Pearl Buck's *The Good Earth*. I learned about our past by reading novels like *Gone with the Wind* and *Huckleberry Finn*. I knew then that the friendship between Huck Finn and Jim was special. I was able to understand what Huck Finn knew all along—friendship transcends race. I remember reading Arthur Miller's play *The Crucible* and thinking that nowhere in my American history textbook was there a discussion of the Salem witch trials. That was the crowning moment when I realized that textbooks and teachers had control over ideas and learning in the classroom. But I was lucky. I had a dad who believed that you couldn't form your own ideas until you had read and thought about the ideas of others. You couldn't know about our history until you had read all our history, regardless of how ugly some of it may be.

I don't remember ever hearing the word *censorship*. But, as I look back, I realize that there was plenty of censorship by omission going on in schools. When I heard discussion in my college children's litera-ture class about whether the monsters in Maurice Sendak's *Where the*

Wild Things Are might scare children, I knew that the people who worried about that didn't know children. I listened to discussions about Garth Williams's *The Rabbit's Wedding* and wondered how we could possibly teach children to celebrate love in all types of families if we didn't allow them to experience it through books.

By the time I became a librarian, I had completely dedicated myself to the ideas and ideals of intellectual freedom. About that time, Judy Blume came into the lives of young adolescent readers. All over the nation, her books were being challenged. But my students were reading her because I was reading her. I was able to lead them to her books because I knew her books. I was able to talk about her books because I understood her books. During this time, I began to realize that having open discussions about books with children and teenagers is the best way to encourage freedom of thought. You teach by example. And I wanted to be an example of free expression. It was also about this time that I began a parent literature program at the middle school where I served as librarian. The idea was to have parents read the same books that their children were reading and to come together once a month to discuss these books. These parents understood that *Blubber* by Judy Blume is a harsh reality of the life of many fifth and sixth graders. But what they also learned was how to discuss this with their children. They began calling me and asking for books about teenage sex and sexuality, death, racism, bullies and the bullied. And we never had a censorship case.

The program for parents paved the way for teachers in this school to branch out and teach novels that have been censored and challenged throughout the nation. These books, like Brock Cole's *The Goats*, Robert Lipsyte's *One Fat Summer*, Jean Craighead George's *Julie of the Wolves*, Katherine Paterson's *Bridge to Terabithia*, Mildred D. Taylor's *Roll of Thunder, Hear My Cry*, and James and Christopher

Collier's *My Brother Sam Is Dead*, are considered classics in the world of children's and young adult literature. But censors don't care. All these books have challenges recorded by the American Library Association's Office for Intellectual Freedom. The teachers and I team-taught these novels, and we looked for powerful novels like Suzanne Newton's *I Will Call It Georgie's Blues* that could make a lasting impact on young readers. It didn't matter to us that Neal Sloan, the main character of the novel, uses profanity to get his mother's attention. It didn't matter that some people might take offense at the way the Reverend Sloan is presented. It didn't matter, because we knew that we could have an open discussion with the students about these issues, and that through that discussion, they would better understand the conflict of the novel and the emotions of the character. I read *The Giver* by Lois Lowry and *The Watsons Go to Birmingham—1963* by Christopher Paul Curtis aloud to a group of seventy-five middle school students who gathered each morning to listen. It was amazing to watch the spontaneous discussion that erupted in the room at the end of each novel. These students had learned how to think and how to express themselves.

These experiences led me to write this book. I really believe that students want to know about their rights. I believe that they have opinions and want to voice them. When adults try to shield readers from ideas that may be controversial, such adults are creating a generation of skeptics and cynics who don't really know the meaning of free speech.

The first edition of this book only included ideas for teaching eleven books for middle school readers that have been challenged or censored somewhere in this nation. This new and revised edition includes nine titles from the first edition and twenty-three new titles appropriate for ages 9–18. Although many more titles could have been included, I have chosen novels that because of their literary merit are most likely to be taught or used in book clubs in public libraries. The ideas for studying the First Amendment remain in this volume but have been used as the Introduction in an effort to set the stage for teaching books that have been banned or challenged. Most readers have a natural interest in their freedom of speech, but most know little about the subject. Perhaps these ideas will encourage parents, public and school librarians, and teachers to make readers aware of how the First Amendment protects their right to read and affects their lives in so many other ways.

The book is divided into six parts: The Bully and the Outcast; Racism and Bigotry; Reality and Tough Choices; Other Cultures and Other Lands; The Past and the Future; and This Was My Life. Each entry includes a summary of the novel, a section called Before Reading, five or six Shared Discussion questions that encourage critical thinking about the overall meaning of the work, and two or three open-ended questions that ask readers to think about the challenges to the novel. There are five suggestions for writing prompts or extension activities to broaden students' knowledge of topics in the novel. In the first edition, there was an extensive annotated bibliography of related fiction and nonfiction that accompanied each entry. This section, now called Read-Alikes, has been shortened to include only five titles. This allows space to include more main entries. At the time of publication, each of these titles is in print. Please note that the bibliographic information refers to the print format. Many of the titles are also available as ebooks and audiobooks.

It is my sincere belief that every time we listen to a student's opinion, we practice the principles of intellectual freedom. This isn't a responsibility for which many of us were prepared by teacher training or in library school. It is a learned responsibility, and it is ours.

It can hardly be argued that either students or teachers shed their constitutional rights to freedom of speech or expression at the schoolhouse gate.

—JUSTICE ABE FORTAS,

TINKER V. DES MOINES INDEPENDENT SCHOOL DISTRICT (1969)

INTRODUCTION

Studying the First Amendment

Too many schools, too many teachers, too many communities are fearful of the one thing that education is supposed to achieve: the capacity to think.

—PETER SCHRAG

This is America! Yet, attempts to ban books from school and public libraries happen on a regular basis. What is amiss in this "land of the free"? Is this censorship war about fear? Control? Power? Is it a fight between the schooled and the unschooled? The sighted and the blind? The thinkers and the nonthinkers? How does this battle affect the education of our children? What kinds of messages are we sending to them regarding their constitutional rights?

When I was in library school, there was a course called Censorship that surveyed such books as *Portnoy's Complaint*, *Of Mice and Men*, and *The Catcher in the Rye*. This was in the days before Sherman Alexie, Judy Blume, Suzanne Collins, Robert Cormier, Robert Lipsyte, J. K. Rowling, Alvin Schwartz, and Ellen Hopkins. It was five years before Steven Pico and his fellow high school students took the Island Trees (New York) school board to court for removing books from the school library. Most library-school students took this censorship course for personal enjoyment; they never realized that fighting censorship could become a very real part of their job.

Today, the battle rages, and public and school librarians are stumbling in their fight to win the war. The enemy is individuals and organized groups, from the right and the left, who are determined to gain power over what the young read, learn, and view. In some cities, school and library boards are under pressure to place ratings on books. In other places, students' names are tagged, at parental request, for restricted use of certain library materials. Frightened librarians are limiting young patrons to the "easy" book section and requiring older readers to bring written parental permission to read such books as Harper Lee's *To Kill a Mockingbird*, Maya Angelou's *I Know Why the Caged Bird Sings*, Pat Conroy's *The Prince of Tides*, and Marjane Satrapi's *Persepolis*. Professionals are self-censoring in the selection process— making every effort to make "safe" choices. These practices, however, aren't eliminating the problem; they are only amplifying the issue.

The problem is obvious. Censors want to control the minds of the young. They are fearful of the educational system because students who read learn to think. Thinkers learn to see. Those who see often question. And young people who question threaten the "blind" and the "nonthinkers." The answer is the classroom. As educators, we cannot, for the sake of the students, allow ourselves to be bullied into diluting the curriculum into superficial facts that do nothing but prepare students for tests. We must talk about the principles of intellectual freedom. We must challenge the young to think about the intent of our forefathers when they wrote the Bill of Rights. We must teach students about their First Amendment rights rather than restrict their use of particular books and materials. And we must encourage them to express their own opinions while respecting the views of others.

By eighth grade, most students can define the Bill of Rights. They can, in a poetic fashion, render a memorized definition of the First Amendment. But do they really know how it affects their lives?

Experience tells me that they don't. As librarians and teachers, we have a task that is much broader than raising public consciousness for First Amendment rights through Banned Books Week exhibits. Our professional role extends beyond removing all restrictions and barriers from the library collection. We must do these things, but we must also accept responsibility for creating a vital connection between the social studies and English curricula by preparing lessons on the First Amendment. We can go into classrooms and engage students in activities and discussion that enable them to think about their personal rights and responsibilities provided by the Constitution. Ask them to read and react to a contemporary novel, such as the graphic novel *Americus* by M. K. Reed or *Property of the Rebel Librarian* by Allison Varnes, that deals with censorship issues. Invite them to apply the situations in the novel to real life. Encourage them to debate the conflict presented in the novels. Then, have them discuss how censorship has affected the writing careers of authors like Jason Reynolds, Laurie Halse Anderson, Chris Crutcher, Chris Lynch, and Jacqueline Woodson. Provide a forum in which students can express their views regarding book censorship and other intellectual freedom issues. And help them understand their personal options regarding the use of books and materials that might offend them. Above all, grant them the opportunity to think, to speak, and to be heard. Schools and libraries that foster this type of open atmosphere send a clear message: the First Amendment is important in school as well as in society at large. Thinkers, regardless of their views, make an important contribution to the American way of life. And thinkers are less likely to become censors.

SHARED DISCUSSIONS

- Read aloud the First and Fourteenth Amendments. Discuss how these two amendments are related.

- Why did our forefathers feel it necessary to include an amendment to the Constitution that guarantees freedom of religion to all Americans? Discuss the relationship between freedom of religion and freedom of expression.
- How would your life be affected if we didn't have the First Amendment?
- Interpret the following quote by Oscar Wilde: "The books that the world calls immoral are the books that show the world its own shame."
- In the Supreme Court case *Island Trees School District v. Pico* (1982), one school board member said, "I would not dream of trying to take that book out of the public library. That would be censorship—and we are not censors." Discuss why removing a book from a school library is censorship. How is the mission of a school library similar to that of a public library? How is it different?
- What is the meaning of "academic freedom"? Why is it important that schools maintain this freedom?
- There are people who think books should have ratings similar to the ones placed on movies and music. How are ratings on any work of art a form of censorship? How do you respond when you see that something is R-rated? Does it trigger your curiosity? What is it about human nature that makes us want to read the books that a person forbids us to read? Suggest ways that a family can deal with controversial books, movies, and music without forbidding their use.
- Elements and topics in books and movies that are often targets of censors are profanity, racism, violence, magic and witchcraft, and sex and sexuality. Some people believe that books with these topics provide "bad" role models for young readers. How might reading these books allow readers the opportunity to better understand these elements in our society and to discuss ways to deal with them?

WRITING PROMPTS AND ACTIVITIES

- Write an essay that explains the following quote by John Morley: "You have not converted a man because you have silenced him."
- Read Ray Bradbury's *Fahrenheit 451* and Lois Lowry's *The Giver*. Write a journal entry discussing how each book is about thought control.
- Read *Annie on My Mind* by Nancy Garden. Use the internet to research the censorship case that occurred with Garden's book in Olathe, Kansas. Write a short journal entry that draws a parallel between the actions of the school administrators in the novel and those of the Olathe school superintendent.
- Research the purpose of the following organizations: the ALA's Office for Intellectual Freedom, the Freedom to Read Foundation, the National Coalition against Censorship, and the Comic Book Legal Defense Fund. Make a brochure describing the mission of each organization. Include contact information. Display the brochures in school and public libraries, and in local bookstores.
- Find out your school district's procedure for dealing with challenged books and materials. Invite a member of the materials review committee or a member of the school board to speak about local book challenges.

READ-ALIKES

Cushman, Karen. *The Loud Silence of Francine Green*. 2019, 256 pp. Houghton Mifflin.

   Ages 9–12. Set in Los Angeles during the McCarthy era, thirteen-year-old Francine Green learns the meaning of free speech when she befriends Sophie Bowman, a nonconformist whose father has been blacklisted by the U.S. government.

Gratz, Alan. *Ban This Book*. 2017. 256 pp. Tom Doherty Associates.

   Ages 9–12. Fourth grader Amy Anne Ollinger takes matters into her own hands when she learns that her favorite book, along with other titles, has been removed from the school library. She operates a banned-books library from her locker and encourages other students to fight for their right to read.

Levithan, David. *Answers in the Pages*. 2022. 176 pp. Knopf, a division of Penguin Random House.

Ages 9–12. Donovan Johnson is in the fifth grade when his mother launches a community-wide campaign to remove a book from her son's classroom because she thinks it promotes homosexuality. At the school board hearing, Donovan and his classmates sit together to support their teacher and the book.

Reed, M. K. *Americus*. 2011. 224 pp. Roaring Brook, an imprint of Macmillan.

Ages 12-up. In this graphic novel, eighth grader Neal Barton battles local Christian activists in an effort to get his favorite fantasy series back on the shelves of the Americus Public Library.

Varnes, Allison. *Property of the Rebel Librarian*. 2018. 288 pp. Random House, an imprint of Penguin Random House.

Ages 9–12. June Harper is in the seventh grade when she launches an effort to fight book censors, a group that includes her parents. She is inspired by a neighborhood lending library and sets up a banned-books library from an abandoned locker in her school.

PART I

THE BULLY AND THE OUTCAST

The desire to belong is a driving need among children and adolescents, and it greatly contributes to their emotional well-being. Their relationship with family and friends and their view of themselves affects who they are and their ability to interact and form relationships with others. Those with body image issues and those who are different in a number of ways often suffer ridicule from their peers and have a difficult time making friends. Bullies prey upon these young people. Some grow up unscathed; others are simply marked victims. The bullies are often peers, but many are adults who contribute to mean behavior and set poor examples to the young. Books about bullying behaviors may serve as a guide to schools and communities as they struggle with this societal problem.

1 Belle Prater's Boy

RUTH WHITE

He was interested in everything and almost
everybody, and the way he looked at things with fresh
eyes made me see them fresh too.

- 1997 NEWBERY HONOR
- SQUARE FISH, AN IMPRINT OF MACMILLAN 2012
- 224 PAGES
- AGES 10–12

Belle Prater has disappeared without a trace. There is no evidence of foul play and no indication that she might have run off with someone else. She simply vanished off the face of the earth. Her sudden disappearance is a mystery to the folks of Coal Station, Virginia, so they spread gossip about her whereabouts. But Belle's only child, Woodrow, is remarkably cool about his mother's vanishing.

After moving in with his Granny and Grandpa Ball, the cross-eyed, gawky, and extremely backward Woodrow uses his storytelling ability to win the hearts of his new classmates. His presence makes school more interesting and life more fun, especially for his first cousin and next-door neighbor, Gypsy Arbutus Leemaster. Gypsy's life is quite the opposite of Woodrow's. Her days are consumed with piano lessons, personal grooming, and instruction in party etiquette. The cousins become fast friends, and when Gypsy has spare time, the two spend time going about town and hanging out in the tree house that Gypsy's father built for her before he died. There are tough moments between the two as well. Gypsy is jealous that Woodrow gets so much attention, whereas she is judged by her looks.

When Belle has been missing a year, Woodrow invites Gypsy to the tree house where he relates his version of what happened to his mother. He had missed some of his clothes and believes that his mother may have left disguised as a boy. As Woodrow reveals his mother's unhappiness, which is likely the reason for her disappearance, Gypsy discovers a secret about her father and learns something very important about herself. Woodrow and Gypsy's story continues in *The Search for Belle Prater* (2005).

BEFORE READING

Pull up images of Appalachia for context while reading. Read aloud descriptive passages from each of the books. Then play a recording of "Appalachian Spring" by Aaron Copland. Discuss how the music relates to the descriptive passages read. Ask your child to share the images that they saw while listening to the music.

SHARED DISCUSSION

- Explain why Gypsy and Woodrow are unlikely friends. Trace the development of their friendship from the beginning of the novel to the end. Which character gains the most from the friendship?
- Describe Woodrow's relationship with his father. How is Grandpa Ball more of a father figure to Woodrow than his real father. What are Gypsy's feelings toward her stepfather, Porter?
- Discuss Love and Belle's relationship as children, teenagers, and adults. How is their relationship connected to Belle's disappearance?
- Gypsy feels abandoned when her father dies; Woodrow suffers from his mother's disappearance. How are Gypsy's feelings different from Woodrow's? How do they help each other come to terms with their losses?
- Love is fanatical about Gypsy's appearance. How does this keep

Gypsy from discovering her true self? Grandpa tells Gypsy, "It's what's in the heart that counts." How does this message influence Gypsy's growth as a character?

- The novel has been challenged because Gypsy's father commits suicide. Why does her father shoot himself in the face? Explain the trauma that Gypsy has faced since that very sad day.
- Some adults are uncomfortable with Woodrow's seemingly "second sense." In the eyes of some people, this is "anti-religious." How does Woodrow's second sense help to define his character and establish the intrigue regarding his mother's disappearance?
- One challenge states that the book isn't "multicultural enough." Draw a comparison between the towns of Coal Station and Crooked Ridge. Discuss what you learn about the Appalachian people. How is this a cultural awakening for readers outside the Appalachian region?

WRITING PROMPTS AND ACTIVITIES

- Write an essay that discusses what Woodrow teaches Gypsy about appearances.
- Write a character sketch of Woodrow from Gypsy's point of view.
- Woodrow is a natural storyteller. In the style of a graphic novel, write and illustrate one of Woodrow's stories.
- Porter Dotson, Gypsy's stepfather, is editor of *The Mountain Echo*, the Coal Station newspaper. Write a news story about Belle Prater's disappearance. Include interviews with Woodrow, Everett Prater, Love Ball Dotson, and Granny and Grandpa Ball.
- Use sites on the internet to find out the functions of the following agencies: Tennessee Valley Authority and the Appalachian Regional Commission. Write a short journal entry that discusses how these agencies have helped the people of Appalachia.

READ-ALIKES

Cleaver, Vera and Bill Cleaver. *Where the Lilies Bloom*. 2001. 224 pp. Trophy Keypoint, an imprint of HarperCollins.

Ages 10–14. Set in Trial Valley in the Great Smoky Mountains, fourteen-year-old Mary Call Luther struggles to care for her three siblings after their father, Roy Luther, dies.

MacLachlan, Patricia. *Journey*. 1993. 112 pp. Yearling, an imprint of Penguin Random House.

Ages 9–12. Eleven-year-old Journey and his sister, Cat, live with their grandparents after their mother left to make a new life for herself. He feels sad and angry and spends his summer vacation searching for clues about her disappearance.

O'Connor, Barbara. *Greetings from Nowhere*. 2015. 224 pp. Square Fish, an imprint of Macmillan.

Ages 9–12. In this novel set at the Sleepy Time Motel in the Great Smoky Mountains of North Carolina, four children on a search for a new life form a friendship with one another.

White, Ruth. *A Month of Sundays*. 2013. 192 pp. Square Fish, an imprint of Macmillan.

Ages 12-up. Garnet is fourteen years old when her mother drops her off with relatives she has never known and strikes out for a fresh start in life.

White, Ruth. *Way Down Deep*. 2011. 224 pp. Square Fish, an imprint of Macmillan.

Ages 9–12. Set in 1944 in Way Down Deep, West Virginia, twelve-year-old Ruby was a toddler when she was abandoned and left in the loving care of Miss Arbutus, the owner of a local boardinghouse. Now that Ruby is older, she searches for information about her family.

2

Blubber

JUDY BLUME

I will act the same as always except I'll just ignore
Wendy. That will teach her a lesson about
threatening people.

- SIMON & SCHUSTER REPRINT EDITION 2014
- 208 PAGES
- AGES 9–12

Fifth grader Jill Brenner has always been an innocent bystander
to mean acts at school until Wendy, the most popular girl in the
class, begins bullying Linda Fischer, an overweight classmate. It
starts when Linda gives a report on whales, and Wendy passes a note
to Caroline and then to Jill that says, "Blubber is a good name for her!"
The girls hold Linda down and reveal her "flowered underpants"; they
cause her to throw up when they force her to eat a chocolate-covered
ant; and they make copies of their "How to Have Fun with Blubber" list
and distribute them to the class. Paper airplanes that say "I'm Blubber—
Fly Me" soar from the rear of the school bus. At times, Jill shows signs
of being uncomfortable with the way Linda is treated, but her desire to
please Wendy is just too strong, and she soon becomes a ringleader.

Things begin to change for Jill when her family attends Warren
Winkler's bar mitzvah, where she is seated at the same table with
Linda Fischer. To Jill's surprise, she and Linda are asked to light the
thirteenth candle on Warren's birthday cake. But Jill is reluctant to
befriend Linda. There is the question about who squealed on Jill and
Tracy for vandalizing Mr. Machinist's mailbox on Halloween. Wendy

tries to convince the girls that Blubber is surely the squealer. At Jill's suggestion, the class puts Linda on trial, but Wendy quickly takes over, bullying her way through the entire event. She doesn't want to give Blubber a lawyer and insists that everything be done her way. At this point, Jill finally takes charge and tells Wendy, "I'm sick of you bossing everyone around."

It's difficult not to be scared of Wendy, but Jill bravely enters the classroom the next morning only to discover that Wendy has adopted Linda as her friend and the entire class has turned on her. She still has Tracy Wu, her oldest and best friend, but there is no one in her class with whom she can eat lunch except for the class loner, Rochelle. As lonely as Jill feels, she does realize, "You sometimes have to make the first move or else you might wind up like Linda—letting other people decide what's going to happen to you."

BEFORE READING

Discuss the familiar saying "Sticks and stones may hurt my bones, but words will never hurt me." Engage your child in a discussion about how words can and do hurt. What is an appropriate response if someone calls you mean names?

SHARED DISCUSSION

- Describe Linda. Why is she such an easy target for bullies like Wendy?
- Brainstorm adjectives that best describe Wendy. How is it obvious that she is the real troublemaker in her class? Jill says, "It's important to be Wendy's friend." Why do the other kids follow Wendy's lead? Explain why Linda is so willing to be Wendy's partner on the class trip.
- Jill is sure that she will win the prize for the most original costume at her school's Halloween parade. She says that the prize doesn't matter

to her, but she likes the idea of winning. Why is winning so important to Jill? Discuss how she feels when she doesn't win the contest.

- Jill tells Tracy that she's not hanging around with Wendy anymore because "she acts like she owns the whole world." Tracy replies, "I've always known that." Discuss why Tracy sees through Wendy long before Jill does.

- Discuss the phrase "Turnabout is fair play." Debate whether Jill gets what she deserves at the end of the novel when Wendy blocks her from using the toilet and calls her "Baby Brenner."

- There are adults who think kids shouldn't read *Blubber* because of the way the kids treat each other. Discuss times that you have witnessed a student bullying another student. Explain why people become bullies. What is the best way to deal with a bully? How does reading about a "real" situation prepare a person for dealing with a similar situation? Why are some adults afraid of discussing "real" issues with kids?

- One of the challenges to *Blubber* concerns the perception that in the book, "bad is never punished. Good never comes to the fore. Evil is triumphant." Discuss whether evil really is triumphant in the book. The novel is about Jill, not Wendy or Linda. What lesson does Jill learn about evil? How is Jill triumphant?

- Some adults disapprove of the novel because of the language that the characters use. Read the passage where Jill talks about cursing, and discuss whether her observation about why people use bad language is true. What is an appropriate response to someone who uses bad language to your face?

WRITING PROMPTS AND ACTIVITIES

- Write an essay that explains why Jill's desire to win the costume contest is the same as her desire to be popular.

- Jill thinks that smashing someone's pumpkins on Halloween isn't right but putting rotten eggs in a person's mailbox is okay. Write a journal entry from Jill's point of view that justifies her thinking. Then write a concluding paragraph that challenges Jill's sense of right and wrong.
- Wendy and Caroline compile a list called "How to Have Fun with Blubber." There are six mean things on the list. Compile a list of six ways to be nice to Linda.
- Define "harassment." Discuss the relationship between harassment and bullying. Most schools have a student handbook that details school rules. Study your child's school handbook. Is there a rule about harassment? Based on your school's rule, discuss whether Linda could have accused her classmates of harassment. Then, role-play a scene in which Linda discusses her problem with the school principal.
- *Blubber* is written in first person from Jill Brenner's point of view. Select a scene from the novel where the kids are especially mean to Linda, and rewrite the scene from Linda's point of view. How does the tone of the scene change? Discuss whether changing the point of view makes the reader more sympathetic to Blubber.

READ-ALIKES

Baskin, Nora Raleigh. *Runt*. 2013. 208 pp. Simon & Schuster.

Ages 10–12. There are many incidents of bullying at Elizabeth's middle school, but she is especially targeted because she is always covered in dog hair, and she smells like the dogs in her mother's in-home kennel. The story chronicles all types of bullying and is told through various perspectives—those of the bully, the bullied, and the bystander.

Hale, Shannon. Illus. by LeUyen Pham. *Real Friends*. 2017. 224 pp. First Second Books, an imprint of Macmillan.

Ages 9–12. This graphic novel is the autobiographical story of Hale and how she deals with losing her best friend to a clique called The Group, led by Jen, the most popular girl in school.

Korman, Gordon. Illus. by Mark Buehner. *The 6th Grade Nickname Game*. 2017. 160 pp. Hyperion.

Ages 9–12. Sixth graders Jeff and Wiley pride themselves in their ability to pick the perfect nickname for everyone in their class, but when they attempt to nickname Cassandra, a new student, things get testy, and their friendship is almost ruined.

Ludwig, Trudy. Illus by Beth Adams. *Confessions of a Former Bully*. 2010. 40 pp. Tricycle Press.

Ages 9–12. Ten-year-old Katie is a bully and is required to meet with the school counselor once week to think about her behavior. She records and illustrates her thoughts about bullying in a notebook.

Palacio, R. J. *Wonder*. 2012. 320 pp. Knopf, an imprint of Penguin Random House.

Ages 9–12. Born with a facial deformity, August "Auggie" Pullman has been homeschooled until his parents decide that at age ten it is time for him to interact with other kids. They enroll him in a private middle school where he endures name-calling and bullying by many of his classmates, but on a class trip he finds that there are those who are willing to show kindness.

3 The Goats

BROCK COLE

"I'm socially retarded for my age," she said with a certain dignity. "Yeah. Me too."

- SQUARE FISH, AN IMPRINT OF MACMILLAN REPRINTED 2010
- 192 PAGES
- AGES 12-UP

Howie, the only child of archaeologists, has traveled the world with his parents, excavating pottery and other artifacts from ancient civilizations. Now that he's thirteen, his parents decide that he needs interaction with boys his own age. Instead of taking him with them to Turkey, they send him to summer camp, where he is teased and taunted by other campers. He is such an outcast that he is named the camp goat.

At a neighboring camp for girls, thirteen-year-old Laura is considered a loner. The only child of a businesswoman whose main interest is climbing the corporate ladder, Laura has spent most of her life alone or surrounded by adults. When she is sent to camp, where she is expected to relate to girls her own age, she becomes acutely aware that she is "socially retarded." She too is named the camp goat.

The tradition at the two camps is to take the goats by boat at night to an island in the middle of the lake, strip them of their clothing, and leave them there alone. The goats are normally retrieved at daybreak, but this time things are different. While Howie and Laura are misfits, the other campers have no clue that these two are bright, courageous young people who will find their own way to fight back. Laura is the first left on the island. When Howie arrives, Laura's quiet whimpering noises lead him to her. He finds her wrapped in an old blanket sitting on a dilapidated tent platform. Frightened and humiliated, Laura listens as Howie unfolds his plan for their escape.

Howie and Laura's simple plan turns into quite an adventure, taking them to a summer cottage and then to a camp for streetwise, underprivileged kids who send them on their way with bellies full of good food. The camp finally notifies Mrs. Golden that her daughter is missing. When she learns of the camp's cruel treatment of Laura and Howie, Mrs. Golden threatens the owners with a lawsuit.

Laura and Howie know that from this day forward, things will be different. They each have a friend, and most importantly, they have learned much about themselves and their ability to survive.

BEFORE READING

Look up the word "goat" in the dictionary. What is the U.S. slang usage of the word? Tell readers that at the West Point Military Academy the lowest-ranked student in the class is called the goat. Explain how the term can be both derogatory and triumphant.

SHARED DISCUSSION

- Howie and Laura are well into their adventure before they learn each other's name. Why do you think they don't introduce themselves by name when they first meet?
- In reference to Parents' Weekend, Mrs. Golden says to Laura, "Well, I'm coming. I mean, if you're having problems, I've got to, haven't I?" Why is Mrs. Golden's reason for coming to Parents' Weekend the wrong reason? How do you think Mrs. Golden contributes to making Laura a misfit?

- Laura and Howie keep a record of the things they have taken so they can pay the people back. How can they possibly repay people they don't even know? Do you think they really intend to repay the people, or does the thought of it simply ease their conscience?

- Sometimes writers use open endings to give readers the opportunity to make up their own mind about what happens. What do you think happens when Laura and Howie find Mrs. Golden? Do they stay at camp for the remainder of the summer? If so, how do the other campers treat them?

- The camp director tries to pass off the incident as a joke. Why would he see humor in humiliating a camper? Explain why cruelty to others is never a joke.

- The novel has been challenged and actually removed from some school libraries because "it contains a passage describing a naked girl." How does stripping the goats of their clothing make the tradition more hateful and disgusting?

- Some adults have labeled *The Goats* as "morally offensive and inappropriate for middle school students." What might be considered "morally offensive" about this book?

- Sometimes, books that make us a little uncomfortable are the ones that make us think about the important issues in life. Discuss how *The Goats* might be considered such a novel. What is life-changing about this book?

WRITING PROMPTS AND ACTIVITIES

- Consider the slang definition of "goat" and write an essay that explains why Howie and Laura are named the goats.

- The novel is written in third person. How would the story change if it were written in first person? Pick a favorite scene in the novel and rewrite it in first person from either Howie's or Laura's point of view.

- Write a television news story about Howie and Laura's disappearance. Then, tape an on-the-spot report when they are found. Include an interview with Howie and Laura, the camp directors, other campers, and Mrs. Golden.
- Write a letter that Howie might send to his parents explaining his experience at camp and why he ran away. Then write a letter that his parents might write to the camp director after hearing from their son.
- Stage a debate about hazing or other camp and school traditions that place people in humiliating and dangerous situations. Include ways to deal with such issues.

READ-ALIKES

Cormier, Robert. *The Chocolate War*. 1974. 264 pp. Ember, an imprint of Penguin Random House.

Ages 12–up. Freshman Jerry Renault takes a ten-day dare from the Vigils, a secret school organization, and refuses to sell chocolate bars for the Trinity High School fundraiser. When the dare is called off, Jerry continues to "disturb the universe" and becomes victim to the Vigils and the corrupt school authorities.

Huang, Charlotte. *Going Geek*. 2016. 304 pp. Delacorte, an imprint of Penguin Random House.

Ages 12–up. Skylar Hoffman, a senior at a preppy boarding school, comes face-to-face with a group of mean girls after she is relegated to a dorm of misfits, a group that she has ignored in the past.

Lynch, Chris. *Slot Machine*. 1995. 241 pp. HarperCollins Children's Books.

Ages 12–up. Elvin isn't athletic and is considered a misfit among his peers, but he is hauled off to a summer retreat with other rising freshman boys at Christian Brothers Academy, where coaches "slot" them into specific sports.

McAnulty, Stacy. ***The Miscalculations of Lightning Girl.*** **2018. 283 pp. Random House, an imprint of Penguin Random House.**

Ages 10–up. Twelve-year-old Lucy, a homeschooled math genius, is academically ready for college, but her grandmother insists that she enroll in public middle school and learn to interact with kids her own age. The students think her weird, but her status improves when she teams up with two classmates to complete a project that calls upon her math skills and ultimately scores the team a "winning" final grade.

Spinelli, Jerry. ***Stargirl.*** **2000. 176 pp. Knopf, an imprint of Penguin Random House.**

Ages 12–up. Stargirl has been homeschooled until tenth grade, when she enters Mica High. For a while, there is a mystique about her, but her weird ways and her unwillingness to follow the crowd soon cause her to be shunned by all the students except Leo Borlock, who falls in love with her.

4 Holes

LOUIS SACHAR

He could hardly lift his spoon during breakfast, and then he was out on the lake, his spoon soon replaced by a shovel.

- 1999 NEWBERY MEDAL
- 1998 NATIONAL BOOK AWARD
- YEARLING, AN IMPRINT OF PENGUIN RANDOM HOUSE 2000
- 272 PAGES
- AGES 10–14

Stanley Yelnats is an overweight middle school kid who is teased and taunted by his classmates. His parents are poor, but they love their only son and support him when he is falsely accused of stealing sneakers. According to Stanley, the sneakers simply "fell out of the sky," and he grabbed them with the intention of giving them to his father, an inventor, who is working on a project that uses old sneakers. Before Stanley can make it home, the police arrest him. It turns out that the sneakers belonged to a famous baseball player who was doing a good deed by donating the shoes to an organization that supports a homeless shelter for children.

When he ends up in court, Stanley believes that he is victim of a curse caused by his "no-good-dirty-rotten-pig-stealing great-great-grandfather." Curse aside, Stanley is given a choice: He can go to jail or serve time at Camp Green Lake, a juvenile detention facility in the middle of a Texas desert. He chooses Camp Green Lake. Having never attended summer camp, Stanley naively believes this to be a new opportunity. He soon learns that there is no lake at Camp Green Lake, and that the campers (inmates) are all juvenile delinquents under the watchful eye of an evil warden who uses the boys to dig holes in search of buried treasure.

Stanley shares a tent with the other boys, and he soon learns the group dynamics. Each boy has a nickname that reveals something about his character, and Stanley is assigned the name Caveman. X-Ray is the leader of the group, and Stanley knows that he must be a friend with the boy if he is to survive.

As the summer progresses, Stanley makes some startling discoveries about himself, the true meaning of friendship, and the ancient curse that has haunted his family for generations. In a parallel story about Stanley's great-great-grandfather, the mystery of the curse is unveiled, and Stanley, in his efforts to help a friend, suddenly finds himself in control of his own destiny and the fate of his unlucky family.

There are two companion novels: *Stanley Yelnats's Survival Guide to Camp Green Lake* (2003) and *Small Steps* (2006).

BEFORE READING

Take time before reading to research juvenile detention centers in your state with your child. Instruct them to investigate the purpose of a juvenile detention center. How does the state work to rehabilitate juvenile offenders? What is the purpose of a probation officer? How is it determined whether a juvenile can be tried as an adult? What are the conditions of most centers?

SHARED DISCUSSION

- Stanley is overweight and considered a misfit by the boys in his school and neighborhood. Discuss why Stanley is an easy target for bullies like Derrick Dunne.
- At what point in the novel does Stanley begin feeling that he belongs to the group of guys at Camp Green Lake?

- Discuss the significance of each boy's nickname. How can nicknames label people and affect the way they feel about themselves? Why does Stanley call Zero by his real name when they are in the desert together?
- Stanley finds out that Zero is the person who stole the Clyde Livingston sneakers. Explain why Stanley is glad that Zero put the sneakers on the parked car. How does the incident change the course of Stanley's life?
- How does Stanley gain courage as the novel progresses? Which other characters at Camp Green Lake show courage? Discuss which characters in the parallel story demonstrate courage.
- The book has been challenged because of profanity. How does the language of some of the guys at Camp Green Lake reflect their character, their environment, and their situation?
- The novel was challenged in an elementary school after a teacher read it aloud to her class. The father bringing the challenge questioned the "morality" of the book. Discuss the reasons why the father thought the book "immoral."
- In reading the book aloud, some teachers choose to omit the profanity. How is omitting language in a novel an act of censorship? What message does this send to students?

WRITING PROMPTS AND ACTIVITIES

- Write a brief article for *Science News* about "Sploosh," the product to eliminate foot odor, invented by Stanley's father. Include comments from Mr. Yelnats that indicate he has intelligence, perseverance, and finally a little luck.
- Write a journal entry that traces the development of Stanley's friendship with Zero. Cite scenes from the novel and use direct quotes to support your thoughts.

- How do the campers (inmates) at Camp Green Lake view Stanley at the end of the novel? Write and illustrate a ten-frame comic strip that presents Stanley as a hero.
- Write two paragraphs that explain why Stanley is given the nickname Caveman.
- Play recordings of several ballads. Ask your child to compare and contrast a musical ballad and a tall tale. Working in small groups, pick one character from the novel and write the lyrics for a ballad about that character. Set the lyrics to a familiar tune and perform the ballad for your full family or a larger group.

READ-ALIKES

Bowling, Dusti. *24 Hours in Nowhere*. 2018. 272 pp. Sterling.

Ages 10–14. Thirteen-year-old Gus lives with his grandmother in the middle of a desert in Arizona. After he is bullied, he teams up with a group of misfits and goes searching for gold that legend says is buried in Dead Frenchman Mine.

Foster, Stewart. *All the Things That Could Go Wrong*. 2018. 336 pp. Little, Brown.

Ages 9–13. Twelve-year-old Alex has OCD, and Dan is harboring a hurt caused when his brother, Ben, was sent to juvenile detention. Other kids bully both boys, and when they work on a project together, the two sworn enemies begin to form a friendship.

Key, Watt. *Alabama Moon*. 2010. 320 pp. Square Fish, an imprint of Macmillan.

Ages 9–12. Ten-year-old Moon has always lived with his father, an antigovernment radical, in rural Alabama. When his father dies, Moon struggles to survive and winds up in reform school.

Pearsall, Shelly. *The Seventh Most Important Thing.* **2015. 288 pp. Knopf, an imprint of Penguin Random House.**

Ages 10–14. Set during the 1960s, Arthur T. Owens lands in court after he hurls a brick and hits the Junk Man in the arm. At the request of the Junk Man, the judge sentences Arthur to 120 hours of community service instead of sending him to juvenile detention.

Vanderpool, Clare. *Moon Over Manifest.* **2010. 368 pp. Delacorte, an imprint of Penguin Random House.**

Ages 9–12. Set in 1936, twelve-year-old Abilene is sent to live in the run-down town of Manifest, where her father grew up, while he rides the rails. Things look bad for Abilene until she discovers a couple of friends and a cigar box with clues that may reveal a solution to an old mystery that haunts the town.

5 Hoot

CARL HIAASEN

Sometimes you're going to be faced with situations where the line isn't clear between what's right and what's wrong. Your heart will tell you to do something different. In the end, all that's left is to look at both sides and go with your best judgment.

- 2003 NEWBERY HONOR
- YEARLING BOOKS, AN IMPRINT OF PENGUIN RANDOM HOUSE 2006
- 292 PAGES
- AGES 9–12

Twelve-year-old Roy Eberhardt is homesick for Montana, where his family lived until his father's job brought them to Coconut Cove, Florida. It's bad enough being the new kid, but Roy has an immediate encounter with seventh grader Dana Matherson, the notorious Trace Middle School bully, who targets his prey on the school bus. When Dana smashes Roy's head against the window, Roy punches him and gets suspended from the school bus for fighting.

One day Roy takes note of a barefoot boy running away from the school bus and across a field. He is curious about the boy, and when he sees him a second time, he follows him. This is how Roy teams up with the boy named Napoleon Bridger, known as Mullet Fingers, and his stepsister, Beatrice. Mullet Fingers is a known vandal and has run away from home because he believes that he is about to be sent to juvenile detention. Roy learns through Beatrice that Mullet Fingers has a very good cause. He enlists the help of Roy and Beatrice, and they launch a plan to save the burrowing owls that are about to become homeless because a Mother Paula's All-American Pancake House is to be built in the field where the owls live.

Their first attempts to halt the construction fail, but Roy and Beatrice recruit their classmates to lodge a protest on the day of the groundbreaking ceremony. Mullet Fingers is there as well. This time he claims he has a bucket full of cottonmouth moccasins that he is about to turn loose. It turns out that his claim is false, but his actions, along with all the other kids' protests, get the attention of many other people, including "Mother Paula" herself.

In the end, the trio is successful because they use their voices and actions to take on construction workers, city politicians, and corporate PR officials to save the owls. Their effort makes national news, the owls are saved, the Mother Paula company donates money to the Nature Conservancy, and Roy discovers a purpose—making a difference for the sake of wildlife and the environment.

BEFORE READING

The U.S. Fish and Wildlife Service is the agency that declares a species endangered. It has classified the burrowing owl as a candidate species. Research with your child to find out what this classification means. Tell them about the Endangered Species Act and the Migratory Bird Treaty Act. Why is it important for the government to have laws that protect animals?

SHARED DISCUSSION

- Discuss how Roy is treated by students at Trace Middle School. Describe his attempts to fit in.
- Roy is bullied by Dana Matherson. At what point does Roy decide he's had enough of Dana's bullying? The vice principal

makes Roy write a letter of apology to Dana. Discuss Dana's reaction when he receives the letter.

- Explain why Roy is upset when he gets the reputation of "tough guy" after he beats up Dana.
- Identify other bullies in the novel. What does Roy learn about bullying when he becomes involved in saving the owls?
- What is Roy's relationship with his parents? How is his family different from Dana's and Mullet Fingers and Beatrice's families?
- Debate whether there is a correlation between Mullet Fingers's home life and his desire to save the owls.
- The novel has been challenged because of profanity. Identify the dialogue in the novel that is troublesome to some people. Explain how profanity defines character.
- Adults have also expressed concern about the "bullying" in the novel. How is bullying a reality in schools? Discuss how bullying might lead to more serious crimes. How does the novel expose bullying and greed on the part of government and large corporations?

WRITING PROMPTS AND ACTIVITIES

- Discuss the term "values in conflict." Write an essay that explains what Roy learns about values in conflict. Use direct quotes from the novel to support your thoughts.
- Write a guest editorial for the Coconut Cove newspaper that Roy might write that explains why he wants to save the burrowing owls.
- Write an essay that explains what Mr. Eberhardt means when he tells Roy that there is a "fine line between courage and stupidity." Quote scenes from the novel to illustrate the difference between courage and stupidity.

- Write a feature story titled "Mother Paula's All-American Pancake House: A Bully" for a national newspaper. Remember to include who, what, when, where, and how.
- Write an acrostic poem from Roy's point of view, using "Bullying" as the spine word.

READ-ALIKES

DeFelice, Cynthia. *Lostman's River*. 2008. 160 pp. Simon & Schuster.

Ages 9–12. Tyler MacCauley lives with his family at Lostman's River, where they engage in a fight to save the wildlife from the greed of those seeking profit from land that surrounds their home.

Hiaasen, Carl. *Chomp*. 2011. 304 pp. Knopf, an imprint of Penguin Random House.

Ages 9–12. Wahoo Cray and his father come face-to-face with a survivalist fraud when they are hired to accompany the star of the *Expedition Survival!* show on a trip through the Everglades.

Hiaasen, Carl. *Flush*. 2005. 272 pp. Knopf, an imprint of Penguin Random House.

Ages 9–12. In the absence of their volatile dad, who cares deeply about the environment, Noah Underwood and his sister, Abbey, take on a casino ship for illegally dumping raw sewage into the ocean.

Hiaasen, Carl. *Scat*. 2009. 384 pp. Knopf, an imprint of Penguin Random House.

Ages 9–12. When their biology teacher goes missing and a fire breaks out in the Everglades, classmates Nick and Marta discover that illegal pipelines, an endangered panther, and a troublemaker called "Smoke" all contribute to the mystery.

Kelly, Lynne. *Song for a Whale*. 2019. 320 pp. Delacorte, an imprint of Penguin Random House.

Ages 9–12. Twelve-year-old Iris is deaf and becomes interested in Blue 55, a hybrid blue/fin whale that is also deaf. Iris records a sound at the frequency the whale can hear, and she and her deaf grandmother travel to Alaska to make a connection with Blue.

TEACHER'S GUIDE

A Complete Teacher's Guide is available on

the publisher's website.

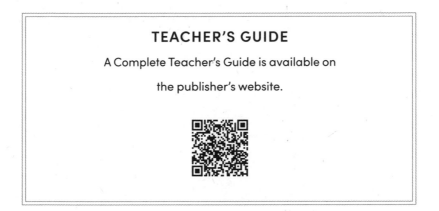

6

When Zachary Beaver Came to Town

KIMBERLY WILLIS HOLT

We watch Paulie hitch the trailer to the back end of his Thunderbird and pull away. Away from the Dairy Maid parking lot. Away from Antler. Away from us.

- 1999 NATIONAL BOOK AWARD FOR YOUNG PEOPLE'S LITERATURE
- SQUARE FISH, AN IMPRINT OF MACMILLAN 2011
- 256 PAGES
- AGES 9–12

Up until the summer of 1971, thirteen-year-old Toby Wilson's life appeared rather ordinary. He and his best friend, Cal, like to roam the small town of Antler, Texas, where they live, escaping the summer heat at Wylie Womack's snow cone stand. Then Paulie Rankin pulls a trailer into town that has the biggest sideshow anyone in Antler has ever seen. For two dollars, a person can see Zachary Beaver, who is considered the fattest boy in the world, weighing in at 643 pounds. Toby and Cal rush in to see the fifteen-year-old Zachary because they are certain this is their only chance to see such a freak show.

Several days later, the trailer is still parked in the parking lot of the Dairy Maid, and Paulie Rankin has left town. Toby and Cal are curious about the fat boy left behind and deliver groceries to the door of the trailer. The town's sheriff is concerned that Zachary has been abandoned and asks for Toby and Cal to help him gather information. The boys attempt to befriend Zachary, but he is reluctant because he isn't accustomed to people being nice to him. He wonders if these are the same boys who asked him rude questions, like "How much do you eat?"

While the trailer remains in Antler, there are other things happening in the lives of Toby and Cal. Toby's mother has gone to Nashville to enter a country music singing contest. When the contest is over and she doesn't come home, Toby struggles with understanding what has happened to his family. He refuses to read any of the letters that his mother sends him.

Cal's family is also dealing with loss. Wayne, Cal's older brother, is killed in Vietnam. The family has flown a U.S. flag every day that Wayne has been at war. Now, Cal's father pulls the entire flagpole out of the ground. Cal regrets that he never wrote his brother letters, Toby doesn't go to Wayne's funeral, and the boys' long friendship is tested.

The thing that brings them back together is Zachary Beaver. The boys learn that Zachary has never been baptized, and they plan a baptism in Gossimer Lake. Zachary Beaver leaves town a few days later and becomes a sideshow in another town. Toby plans a trip to see his mother, and Toby and Cal end the summer having learned important lessons about the power of friendship.

BEFORE READING

Engage your child in a discussion about the true qualities of friendship. Have them create a list of the things that they have in common with their best friend and the things they may disagree on. Allow time for them to share their list. Ask them what the phrase "unlikely friendship" means. Discuss the fact that sometimes people from different backgrounds can still be friends. How might an unlikely friendship change a person's life?

SHARED DISCUSSION

- Toby and Cal have been friends for a long time. How does Cal need Toby when Wayne dies? Discuss whether Cal is more upset with Toby because of the letter he wrote to Wayne or because Toby didn't attend Wayne's funeral.

- Reread the dialogue exchanged between Toby and his dad when they are fishing. How do Mr. Wilson's words explain what has happened to their family? Discuss whether this talk helps Toby better understand his father and the decisions he has made.
- Explain how Toby's decision to read all the unread letters from his mother is symbolic of his acceptance that she isn't coming home.
- When Zachary Beaver first comes to town, Toby and Cal see him as a freak—a sideshow. At what point in the novel do the boys begin to see Zachary as a friend?
- Why does it take Zachary so long to warm up to the boys?
- The novel has been challenged because of "sexual content." Which scenes might bring such a complaint? Debate whether it's Toby's adolescent yearning for Scarlett. How is this normal for a thirteen-year-old boy?
- Some adults are troubled that Toby lies so much. Why does he tell lies when people around town ask him about his mother? Discuss whether the lies are a way Toby deals with the reality that his mother has left them.
- People have voiced concerns with the name-calling and bullying in the novel. When Zachary Beaver rolls into town in his trailer that is decorated with lights, people shout things like "Fatty, fatty, two by four. Can't get through the kitchen door." They also ask embarrassing questions, like "How much do you eat?" Discuss whether these are the words of bullies or simply rude people. Explain why Toby is so sensitive to the way Zachary is being treated. How does Zachary deal with such name-calling?

WRITING PROMPTS AND ACTIVITIES

- Write two paragraphs that explain why Toby writes a letter to Wayne and signs Cal's name.

- Write a letter that Toby writes to his mother at the end of the novel. What does he tell her about the summer? What does he say about her leaving home? What does he say about himself and how he has been doing?
- Miss Myrtie Mae is the town historian and librarian. Write an article that she might write for the town scrapbook about Zachary Beaver.
- Based on information garnered from the novel, write a journal entry about the attitude of Wayne and his family about the Vietnam War. Cite passages from the novel to support your thoughts.
- Toby changes during the summer of 1971. Write a brief journal entry that discusses the changes within Toby from the beginning of the novel to the end. What does he learn about himself? What is Zachary's role in Toby's self-discovery? Use direct quotes and cite passages from the novel to support your thoughts.

READ-ALIKES

Frank, Steven B. *Armstrong & Charlie*. 2017. 298 pp. Houghton Mifflin Harcourt.

Ages 10–14. Set in 1974 in Hollywood Hills, California, Charlie, a white boy, is grieving the death of his brother while Armstrong, a Black boy, is angry about being bused to a formerly all-white school. As the two sixth graders approach graduation, they manage to shed their differences and form a special friendship.

Holt, Kimberly Willis. *Dancing in Cadillac Light*. 2003. 176 pp. Puffin, an imprint of Penguin Random House.

Ages 9–12. It's 1968, and eleven-year-old Jaynell Lambert is excited about the summer and some of the changes coming to her town of Moon, Texas. When her grandfather arrives in his Cadillac convertible, she becomes curious about his frequent visits to a poor family in town.

Schmidt, Gary D. *The Wednesday Wars*. **2007. 272 pp. Houghton Mifflin Harcourt.**

Ages 9–12. Set in the late 1960s when families are torn apart by the raging war in Vietnam and peace movements at home, seventh grader Holling Hoodhood endures every Wednesday afternoon with a teacher who doesn't like him. A 2008 Newbery Honor book.

Stead, Rebecca. *Liar & Spy*. **2012. 208 pp. Wendy Lamb Books, an imprint of Penguin Random House.**

Ages 9–12. Seventh grader Georges is an outsider at school and a newcomer to the apartment building where he lives with his family. He meets Safer, a strange boy who claims to be a spy, and gets caught up in his mysterious capers. Both boys learn how to be a friend.

Williams-Garcia, Rita. *One Crazy Summer*. **2010. 224 pp. Amistad, an imprint of HarperCollins.**

Ages 9–12. This 2011 Newbery Honor book is set in 1968 in Oakland, California, where the three Gaither sisters travel to see the mother who abandoned them. Eleven-year-old Delphine tells the story about their crazy summer when they learn about the Black Panthers, peace movements, and their mother.

7 Wringer

JERRY SPINELLI

For much of his life Palmer LaRue had felt he was standing at the edge of a black, bottomless hole. On the fifty-ninth day before his tenth birthday, he fell in.

- 1998 NEWBERY HONOR
- HARPERCOLLINS 1997
- 240 PAGES
- AGES 10–UP

Set in the small town of Waymer, Palmer LaRue is dreading the day that he turns ten. Each year, the town raises money for the community park by sponsoring a Family Fest. There are rides, a pie-eating contest, and food for everyone, but the highlight of the week-long event is Pigeon Day. Men pay a fee to shoot pigeons as ten-year-old boys rush in to wring the necks of the wounded birds. To most men and boys in Waymer, this is an initiation ceremony—a rite of passage.

Palmer isn't like the other boys. He's more sensitive and doesn't make friends easily. To his surprise, three local bullies anoint him with gifts on his ninth birthday and give him the nickname Snots. The day is made even more special when Farquar gives him "the treatment." His mother protests when she sees the dark bruise on his arm, but his dad seems proud of it. Then there is the issue with his dad's sharp-shooter trophy, which he proudly displays on the mantel. His mother tries to ignore it, and Palmer sees it as a constant reminder of his role on Pigeon Day, when he turns ten.

When a pigeon shows up on his windowsill, Palmer adopts it and names it Nipper. The closer he becomes to Nipper, the more he realizes that he isn't cut out to be a wringer. He hides the pigeon from the guys but eventually tells Dorothy, a neighborhood friend whom he had ditched in favor of the gang. Dorothy understands and vows to help Palmer save Nipper.

Dorothy takes Nipper to the railroad yard and sets him free. In horror, Palmer realizes that is the location where the pigeons are captured for Pigeon Day. Finally it is the day of the shoot, and Palmer witnesses Nipper being shot. He defies peer pressure and rushes in to scoop up the wounded bird. He courageously walks across the field with the bloody bird in his arms and takes him home. Palmer's father is very proud.

BEFORE READING

Discuss the qualities of a hero. What is the relationship between courage and heroism? Explain why it is more difficult to be a hero than to follow along with the crowd. How is a courageous person almost always a winner?

SHARED DISCUSSION

- "He did not want to be a wringer" is the opening sentence of the novel. Explain why Palmer is reluctant to participate in Pigeon Day when he is expected to be a wringer. Compare his feelings with those of most other ten-year-old boys in his town. What is his father's attitude toward Pigeon Day? Debate whether Palmer feels pressure to become a wringer because his father was a champion sharpshooter.

- Describe Beans, Mutto, and Henry. Why is it so important for Palmer to be accepted by them? Explain Palmer's mother's reaction to the gang. How does Beans become the leader of the group? How is Henry different from the other boys? Explain what Palmer means by "He saw in Henry something of himself, and worse, what he could become." What is the purpose of "the treatment"?

- Dorothy is younger than Palmer, but he has always been her friend. Discuss how he treats Dorothy after Beans, Mutto, and Henry have accepted him into the gang. What turn of events causes Palmer to accept Dorothy's friendship again? How does she contribute to the resolution of the internal conflict that Palmer suffers?

- How is Nipper's arrival on Palmer's windowsill a reminder of the dreaded Pigeon Day? Palmer thinks that he is hiding Nipper. At what point do his parents learn that he has a pigeon in his room?

- Palmer becomes the boy who does crazy things at school. Explain his sudden change in behavior. How does his behavior elevate him in the eyes of his classmates? Discuss why some students cheer bad behavior.

- The novel has been challenged for "violence." Discuss why the town has made the shooting of pigeons an annual event. What are the citizens teaching boys when they expect them to be wringers? Explain what Spinelli is saying about violence by writing this novel. How should people who are concerned about violence focus on the character of Palmer and his ultimate willingness to refuse to participate?

- Farquar is a legendary wringer. He is also the guy who gives boys "the treatment" on their birthday. Why do censors object to the treatment? Compare and contrast Palmer's mother's and father's reactions to the treatment. What message is Palmer sending when he refuses the treatment later in the novel?

- There have also been challenges to the novel because of "animal cruelty." Discuss Palmer's effort to protect Nipper. When Palmer rescues his wounded pigeon, a young child asks, "Can I have one too, Daddy?" Discuss Palmer's influence on the younger generation in terms of how animals should be treated.

WRITING PROMPTS AND ACTIVITIES

- "Nipper's toes clutched and moved on his scalp, and for a strangely wonderful moment he felt himself crowned." Write a journal entry that explains why Palmer feels "crowned."

- In the eyes of guys like Beans and the gang, Palmer is a coward. Write a journal entry that discusses his act of courage when he refuses to be a wringer. Cite passages and use direct quotes from the novel to support your thoughts.

- Palmer finds the courage to expose his feelings about Pigeon Day. Write a letter to the editor of the Waymer newspaper that Palmer might write detailing why Pigeon Day is violent and blatantly cruel to animals.

- Trace Palmer's growth as a character from the beginning of the novel to the end. Then write a short journal entry that discusses the man-against-self conflict. Include a concluding paragraph about the resolution.

- Think about Palmer's father's thoughts about Pigeon Day. Why do you think he changed his thoughts about Pigeon Day? Write a brief journal entry that explains the symbolism of the missing golden bird from the mantel at Palmer's house.

READ-ALIKES

Andrews, Ryan. *This Was Our Pact.* 2019. 336 pp. Roaring Brook, an imprint of Macmillan.

> Ages 10–14. In this graphic novel, Ben and his friends form a pact to find out where the paper lanterns end up after the community floats them down the river during the annual Autumn Equinox Festival. The day comes, and the boys set out on their bikes, but Nathaniel, a kid who doesn't fit in with the gang, breaks the pact and turns back.

Law, Ingrid. *Savvy.* **2010. 368 pp. Puffin, an imprint of Penguin Random House.**

Ages 10–14. It's a rite of passage for each Beaumont to receive their supernatural ability known as savvy when they turn thirteen. Twelve-year-old Mississippi (Mibs) is anticipating her next birthday but is also a little frightened because she realizes that savvy has caused problems for her family.

Salazar, Aida. *The Moon Within.* **2019. 240 pp. Arthur A. Levine Books, an imprint of Scholastic.**

Ages 9–12. In this novel written in verse, eleven-year-old Celi Rivera is resisting the ancient Mexica ritual of the moon ceremony that marks the day of a girl's first period. Her mother and other women in the community believe in this tradition, but Celi is more interested in living a more contemporary life, one that includes repairing her friendship with Mar and recognizing Mar's issues related to gender identity.

Spinelli, Jerry. *Fourth Grade Rats.* **1993. 96 pp. Scholastic.**

Ages 8–10. This humorous novel about rebellious boys who become "rats" when they enter fourth grade chronicles the transformation of a group of friends who seem determined to make everyone's life miserable. Suds, the sensitive one, feels guilty and really doesn't have the heart of a "rat."

Spinelli, Jerry. *Hokey Pokey.* **2014. 320 pp. Yearling, an imprint of Penguin Random House.**

Ages 9–12. This coming-of-age novel is set in a place called Hokey Pokey, where there are no adults, and kids race their bicycles and play in areas with names like "Tantrums" and cherish labels like "Snotsippers." Jack, the main character and most popular big kid, wakes up one day and realizes that it is time. Only he recognizes what that means.

8

One Fat Summer

ROBERT LIPSYTE

I always hated summertime. When people take off
their clothes. In winter you can hide yourself.... But
in the summertime they can see your thick legs and
your wobbly backside and your big belly and your soft
arms. And they laugh.

- HARPERCOLLINS 2004
- 153 PAGES
- AGES 12-UP

Fourteen-year-old Bobby Marks is doomed to spend the summer
with his family at Rumson Lake, a community where many New
Yorkers go to escape the heat and the fast-paced life of the city.
To overweight Bobby, the lake means swimming. Swimming means
taking off your clothes. Taking off your clothes means revealing your
fat body to the local Rumson boys so they can call you names like
"Crisco Kid."

Bobby's only plan for the summer is to complete a school project
with Joanie, his best friend and supporter. To his surprise, Joanie mys-
teriously returns to the city, leaving him with nothing to do but to sit
around and feel sorry for himself. Mr. Marks has ideas of how Bobby
should spend his summer, but Bobby rejects all of his dad's suggestions. Instead, he secretly takes a job as a yard boy for Dr. Kahn, who
turns out to be a bully. The summer is looking better, especially when
Bobby realizes that physical labor is causing him to lose weight.

Then Willie Rumson, a jobless town bum, decides he wants
Bobby's job. When Bobby refuses to relinquish the job, Willie
threatens to gun him down. At this point, Bobby's newly discovered

confidence is put to the test. With only a rusty Cub Scout knife in his pocket for defense, Bobby takes on Willie in an underwater fight. Willie, who is not used to losing, is surprised when Bobby, an excellent swimmer, defeats him without ever using the knife. This autobiographical story continues in *Summer Rules* (1981) and *The Summerboy* (1982).

BEFORE READING

One Fat Summer is an autobiographical coming-of-age novel. Discuss the term "coming-of-age." At what age do most young adults begin their journey to adulthood? Make a list of the physical and emotional characteristics that identify coming-of-age.

SHARED DISCUSSION

- "Rule number one: never let people know they can get to you or they'll never stop trying." Find incidents in the novel where Bobby lets people get to him.
- Bobby doesn't tell his parents about his job. At what point does Bobby discover that his mother knows about the yard job? How does Bobby explain his need for secrecy?
- Dr. Kahn advertises the lawn job for one dollar per hour but offers Bobby only seventy-five cents an hour. Why does Bobby accept the job? Why do you think Dr. Kahn keeps Bobby on if he is so dissatisfied with his work? What makes Bobby continue to work when he takes so much verbal abuse from Dr. Kahn?
- Why does Pete jump Willie when the problem between Bobby and Willie has been solved? Why do Bobby and Michelle hate Pete for his actions? What does Bobby mean when he says, "Pete didn't know any more about being a man than I did"?
- When Bobby's mother doesn't notice his weight loss, he says, "She

didn't really look at me. Nobody really looks at people in their own house." In what other ways are Bobby's parents blind to things in his life? Debate whether Bobby's statement is true in most families.

- Some adults have challenged the novel because of one scene that they call "sexually explicit." To what scene are they referring? How does this scene symbolize a "sexual awakening" for most adolescents?

- The novel has also been challenged because of "violence." How does the violence reveal Willie Rumson's character? Explain how the fight at the end of the novel contributes to Bobby's journey toward manhood.

- There have been other challenges to the novel because of the "derogatory terms for Blacks, Jews, and Italians." Discuss these ethnic slurs in context of the time and place of the novel. What causes people to develop prejudices and to resort to name-calling? Why is it important to develop tolerance and an understanding of others?

WRITING PROMPTS AND ACTIVITIES

- Willie Rumson and Dr. Kahn are both bullies. Write a brief journal entry that contrasts their bullying styles.

- Bobby makes up stories about heroes. Write a short story in which Bobby Marks is the hero.

- Pretend that Bobby visits a support group for overweight teens. Prepare and deliver a speech that Bobby might give at the end of the novel when he has lost weight.

- Bobby's friend Joanie asks, "Are you a man or a rug?" Write a journal entry that chronicles Bobby's journey from "rug" to "man." Cite specific scenes and direct quotes from the novel to support your thoughts.

- Consider these qualities of a classic: expresses life, truth, and beauty; stands the test of time; possesses universal appeal; and demonstrates relevance to multiple generations of readers. *One Fat Summer* was first published in 1977. Write a journal entry that expresses why it is considered a classic.

READ-ALIKES

Baron, Chris. *All of Me*. 2019. 312 pp. Feiwel & Friends, an imprint of Macmillan.

> Ages 9–12. This novel in verse is the story of Ari, an overweight boy who moves cross-country with his parents and runs head-on into bullies. He becomes friends with two outcasts and along the way finds himself changing, both inside and out.

Going, K. L. *Fat Kid Rules the World*. 2004. 224 pp. Penguin, an imprint of Penguin Random House.

> Ages 12-up. Seventeen-year-old Troy Billings is friendless and weighs in at 296 pounds. He is about to end his miserable life by jumping on to the subway track when a homeless teenager steps up and saves him.

Lange, Erin Jade. *Butter*. 2012. 304 pp. Bloomsbury.

> Ages 12-up. Butter, a sixteen-year-old obese boy, is lonely and targeted by bullies. He gains the attention of his peers when he vows to eat himself to death live on the internet.

Mackler, Carolyn. *The Earth, My Butt, and Other Big Round Things*. 2018. 288 pp. Bloomsbury.

> Ages 12-up. Fifteen-year-old Virginia Shreves is an overweight misfit in a dysfunctional family that cares only about body image and success. She becomes friends with overweight Froggy Welsh, who helps her gain the self-confidence she needs to stand up to her "pushy" mother.

Marino, Peter. *Dough Boy.* **2005. 176 pp. Holiday House.**

Ages 12–up. Fifteen-year-old Tristan has never been bothered by his weight until Kelly, the health-conscious daughter of his mother's boyfriend, moves in. Though intimidated by her at first, Tristan decides he's had enough of her bullying and finds the courage to stand up to her.

PART II

RACISM AND BIGOTRY

R acism and bigotry are very real problems in our society. Children and teens have never experienced the overt seg- regation in schools and public places that existed before the Civil Rights Movement, but they are aware of different types of racial injustice that have reached epidemic levels in cities and communities across the nation. Whether it's violence in the streets of Charlottesville or the murder of unarmed Black teens, these acts of racism affect the lives of the young, and they need to know their role in stopping these horrific acts of carnage at the hands of law enforcement officers. At the same time, they need to make an all-important connection between past efforts to change racial inequalities with today's issues related to racism. Books about such racial injustices are the best way to have open conversations with the young so that they may find their voices in effecting change.

9

Roll of Thunder, Hear My Cry

MILDRED D. TAYLOR

We consequently found ourselves comical objects to cruel eyes that gave no thought to our misery.

- 1977 NEWBERY MEDAL
- PENGUIN, AN IMPRINT OF PENGUIN RANDOM HOUSE 2001
- 304 PAGES
- AGES 9–12

Set during the Great Depression in Mississippi, the Logan family struggles against poverty and the risk of losing their most cherished possession—four hundred acres of rich farmland. Three generations of Logans live under one roof on the land that Grandpa Logan purchased in 1887. Now, the Logans are in trouble. For three years, their cotton crop hasn't brought in enough income to pay the expenses of the farm, and Harlan Granger, the white man whose family once owned the Logan land, is set on getting the land back and rebuilding the original Granger plantation.

Told from the point of view of nine-year-old Cassie, the Logans' story begins in October, when the crops are in and the Black children start their school year. David Logan, Cassie's father, is away in Louisiana, laying track for the railroad to earn extra cash to pay the farm debts. Big Ma Logan, now in her sixties, is left in charge of running the household, while Mary Logan, Cassie's mother, teaches at the Black school and manages the farm. The Logan children are too young to appreciate the value of the land and their father's intense effort to save it. But they are old enough to realize the racial discrimination that envelops their life. When Stacey and Cassie go with Big Ma to a nearby small town to sell milk and eggs, Cassie is the victim of several acts of racism. In Mr. Barnett's store, she is forced to wait until the white customers have been helped, and Lillian Jean Simms, a white girl, blocks Cassie's path on the sidewalk and demands that Cassie apologize for trying to pass her. Then, as the Logan children make their daily walk to the Great Faith Elementary and Secondary School, they are splattered with mud by the school bus that takes the white children to the Jefferson Davis County School.

Just as the Logan children are struggling to understand the injustice of the school system, more serious acts of racism erupt in their lives. The threat of the night riders is looming, and Mary Logan is fired from her teaching position for lodging a protest against the "old" and "worn-out" textbooks that once belonged to the white school. Then, the Wallaces, owners of a local store, badly burn some of the sharecroppers. When Papa comes home to help organize a boycott of the Wallaces' store, he is shot in the leg and loses his job with the railroad.

The Logan family story continues in *Song of the Trees* (1975), *Let the Circle Be Unbroken* (1981), *The Road to Memphis* (1990), and *The Well: David's Story* (1995).

BEFORE READING

Read aloud "The Negro Mother" by Langston Hughes. Discuss the living conditions for African Americans in the South in the 1930s. Then analyze Hughes's poem. What does Hughes mean when he makes reference to "the long dark way"? Why does he think it is important for people to understand the past?

SHARED DISCUSSION

- The white children begin their school year in August, but the Black children don't start school until October. Explain why the school calendar is different for the Black children.

- Mary Logan is fired from her teaching position for lodging a protest against the secondhand textbooks. Why do the other teachers at the Black school call her a "disruptive maverick"? Explain what Miss Crocker means when she tells Mary that she is "biting the hand that feeds her."

- The bus driver likes to entertain his white passengers by splattering mud on the Black children as they walk the dirt roads to school. Discuss what the Black children do to get back at the bus driver.

- Describe Cassie's day when Big Ma finally invites her to go into town. Why does Big Ma make Cassie apologize to Lillian Jean for an incident that isn't Cassie's fault? How does Cassie eventually get back at Lillian Jean?

- How is Jeremy Simms different from other members of his family? Why does he befriend the Logan children?

- Why do Cassie's parents organize a boycott of the Wallaces' store? Explain why boycotting is difficult for people like Mr. Turner.

- The novel has been challenged in schools across the country because of its depiction of racial bias. Discuss the difference between racial bias and racial discrimination. How do racial bias and racial discrimination reveal the ills of society?

- Why is it important to understand rather than deny that discrimination exists? What is your role in eliminating any type of discrimination in your school and community?

WRITING PROMPTS AND ACTIVITIES

- Write a brief journal entry that interprets the title of the novel. What is the "thunder"? What is the "cry"?
- Think about the qualities of a hero. Then write a journal entry that reveals the heroic characteristics of Mary and David Logan.
- Discuss the difference between civil liberties and civil rights. Write an essay that explains how the Logans' civil liberties and rights are violated. Use direct quotes and cite specific scenes to support your thoughts.
- Locate poems by Langston Hughes and discuss his style. In his style, write a poem about the Logan family titled "The Long Dark Way."
- The 1964 Civil Rights Act was the strongest civil rights bill in U.S. history. Research the provisions of this act. Write a journal entry that discusses the many ways this act changed the lives of minorities in the United States.

READ-ALIKES

Armstrong, William H. Illus. by James Barkley. *Sounder*. 1969. 116 pp. HarperCollins.

　　Ages 10-up. The nameless boy's father is a sharecropper, but times are hard. When the father steals some meat to feed his hungry family, he is arrested and taken to prison, leaving the boy to be the man of the family.

Burg, Shana. *A Thousand Never Evers*. 2009. 320 pp. Yearling, an imprint of Penguin Random House.

　　Ages 10-up. Set in Kuckachoo, Mississippi, in 1963, Addie Ann Picket attends a segregated school and comes face-to-face with violence when her older brother runs away to escape the KKK.

Cline-Ransome, Lesa. *Finding Langston*. 2018. 112 pp. Holiday House.

　　Ages 9–12. Set in 1946, Langston's world is shattered when his mother dies and his father moves the two of them from their rural Alabama home to Chicago, where he finds a job in a paper plant. Langston, who is taunted by bullies, finds refuge in the public library.

Spinelli, Jerry. *Maniac Magee*. 1999. 192 pp. Little, Brown.

Ages 9–12. Orphan Jeffrey "Maniac" Magee runs away from the troubled home of his aunt and uncle and ends up in the racially divided town of Two Mills, Pennsylvania. He struggles to find a home, but when he faces off with Mars Bar, he not only finds a place to live, but he manages to close the racial gap in the town.

Tillage, Leon Walter. Illus. by Susan L. Roth. *Leon's Story*. 2000. 112 pp. Square Fish, an imprint of Macmillan.

Ages 9–12. Leon tells about the years that his father was a sharecropper and how the family lived in fear of the Ku Klux Klan.

The Watsons Go to Birmingham—1963

CHRISTOPHER PAUL CURTIS

I ain't never heard of no sickness that makes you kill little girls just because you don't want them in your school. I don't think they're sick at all, I think they just let hate eat them up and turn them into monsters.

- 1996 NEWBERY HONOR
- DELACORTE, AN IMPRINT OF PENGUIN RANDOM HOUSE 1995
- 210 PAGES
- AGES 10-UP

Ten-year-old Kenny Watson is bullied by his older brother Byron, an "official juvenile delinquent." Kenny, an excellent student, is quiet and serious. He is attentive to his younger sister, Joetta, and is extremely sensitive to the needs and problems of his friends. Thirteen-year-old Byron has already failed two grades and is making no progress toward improvement. Instead of devoting time to schoolwork, Byron spends his free time finding out how much trouble he can create at home and at school. Kenny seems to be the best target for Byron and his gang until Rufus Fry moves to the Watsons' neighborhood. Like Kenny, who is burdened with being smart and having a lazy eye, Rufus has two things going against him. Being from the South, he speaks with a southern drawl, and his clothes are tattered and torn. Kenny and Rufus become soulmates until one day Kenny forgets what real friendship is about and joins in when the kids on the school bus laugh at the clothes Rufus Fry is wearing. When Kenny finally gets the nerve to tell his mother how he has hurt Rufus, Mrs. Watson walks Kenny to the Frys' house and helps Kenny make amends.

Mrs. Watson doesn't seem to have the same skill in dealing with Byron. In fact, she is so disgusted with his behavior that she and Mr. Watson decided to deliver Byron to Grandma Sands in Birmingham, Alabama. The deal is that Byron will stay in Birmingham for the summer, and if there is no change in his behavior, he will extend his stay through the following school year.

Two things happen in Birmingham that change the purpose of the Watsons' trip. Kenny, ignoring a No Swimming sign, almost drowns and is rescued by Byron. Grateful that Byron pulls him from the "Wool Pooh," Kenny is amazed when he sees his brother shake and break into sobs, an uncharacteristic behavior for Byron. Then, all the news stories about the political and social problems in the South are made real when a church in Grandma Sands's neighborhood is bombed. Thinking that Joetta, the youngest Watson, is a casualty at the church, the frightened Watsons run from the house in search of the little girl. Though Joetta is safe, Mr. and Mrs. Watson take their three children and leave that night, swearing to tell no one what they witnessed in Birmingham.

Kenny is the person who suffers the most from the memories of the trip. As he sits in the bathroom sobbing and replaying the scene of the bombing, Byron assures him, "There ain't nothing wrong with being sad or scared about that. I'm sad about it too. I got real scared too."

BEFORE READING

Guide your child to do some independent research to find out about events related to the Civil Rights Movement in 1963. Make a timeline of the most significant events. Discuss these events and why they were important to the social issues of the time.

SHARED DISCUSSION

- Discuss the conflict of the novel. How do the near-tragic incidents contribute to the resolution of the conflict?

- The kids make fun of Kenny because he is smart. How do Kenny's teachers make things worse for him? Discuss the reasons why being smart should be "cool."

- The bus driver tells Rufus, "Don't you pay no mind to them little fools, they ain't happy lest they draggin' someone down." Why do people feel the need to "drag others down"? Discuss why Kenny feels guilty that he joined with the other kids to taunt Rufus.

- Explain what Mrs. Watson means when she says that in Birmingham, "Things aren't perfect, but people are more honest about the ways they feel."

- What does Mrs. Watson do to prepare her children for the trip to Birmingham? Discuss the things that she cannot prepare them for. Explain why Mrs. Watson doesn't want to tell anyone in Flint what her family witnessed in Birmingham.

- The book has been challenged because of profanity. How does this language define character and create in the reader an emotional response to the situation?

- Others have challenged the novel because of its violence. Curtis draws on the real event of the bombing of the 16th Street Baptist Church in Birmingham. How is this a pivotal moment in the novel? Explain how this violent act changes the Watsons, especially Byron and Kenny. Draw a connection between the violence in Curtis's novel and the racial violence in our country today.

- Some parents have complained about the novel because they don't want their children to know that the Civil Rights Movement ever existed. Can there be change if we don't first understand the past?

WRITING PROMPTS AND ACTIVITIES

- Write a journal entry that reveals the central theme of the novel. Make specific references to the book to support your thoughts.
- Find out about the students who integrated Central High School in Little Rock, Arkansas, in 1957. Write a letter that Kenny Watson might write to these students after his trip to Birmingham in 1963.
- Write a short journal entry that discusses why not knowing about the civil rights era is more dangerous than knowing about it.
- In the Epilogue to *The Watsons Go to Birmingham—1963*, Christopher Paul Curtis writes, "It is almost impossible to imagine the courage of the first African American children who walked into segregated schools or the strength of the parents who permitted them to face the hatred and violence that awaited them. They did it in the name of the movement, in the quest for freedom." Prepare a dramatic tribute to these children. Include poetry, songs, excerpts from civil rights speeches, and original compositions.
- The bombing of the 16th Street Baptist Church in Birmingham, Alabama, took place on September 15, 1963. Locate newspaper articles about this tragic event. Who were the people responsible for the bombing? How long did it take to bring them to trial? Then write and illustrate a chapter for a graphic novel about the civil rights era that documents the horror of the 16th Street Baptist Church bombing.

READ-ALIKES

Beals, Melba Pattillo. *March Forward, Girl: From Young Warrior to Little Rock Nine*. 2018. 224 pp. Houghton Mifflin Harcourt.

   Ages 9–12. Beals relates her story of growing up in Jim Crow Arkansas and her plight to become one of the famous Little Rock Nine, the students who integrated Central High School in Little Rock.

Freedman, Russell. *Freedom Walkers: The Story of the Montgomery Bus Boycott.* **2006. 112 pp. Holiday House.**

Ages 9–up. Documented with personal stories and black-and-white photographs, Freedman presents the everyday people and heroes involved in the Montgomery, Alabama, event that was the start of the Civil Rights Movement.

Levine, Kristin. *The Lions of Little Rock.* **2013. 320 pp. Penguin, an imprint of Penguin Random House.**

Ages 9–12. Set in Little Rock, Arkansas, in 1958, thirteen-year-old Marlee becomes friends with Liz, a light-skinned Black girl passing as white. When Liz is forced to leave school because the school district refuses to integrate, the two girls meet secretly until their friendship becomes unsafe for both girls.

Lewis, John, and Andrew Aydin. Illus. by Nate Powell. *March: Book Three.* **2016. 256 pp. Top Shelf Productions.**

Ages 12–up. In this third book in the graphic novel memoir trilogy that documents his work with the Civil Rights Movement, the late Congressman John Lewis covers the bombing of the 16th Street Baptist Church along with other acts of terror during this volatile time in the nation's history.

Scattergood, Augusta. *Glory Be.* **2014. 208 pp. Scholastic.**

Ages 9–12. Set in 1964 in Hanging Moss, Mississippi, Gloriana Hemphill is denied her twelfth birthday celebration at the community pool when the town's politicians close the whites-only pool after freedom people from the North threaten to integrate it.

11 Monster

WALTER DEAN MYERS

ILLUSTRATED BY CHRISTOPHER MYERS

Sometimes I feel like I have walked into the middle of a movie. Maybe I can make my own movie. The film will be the story of my life. No, not my life, but of this experience. I'll call it what the lady who is the prosecutor called me. MONSTER.

- MICHAEL L. PRINTZ AWARD 2000
- AMISTAD, AN IMPRINT OF HARPERCOLLINS 2019
- 336 PAGES
- AGES 14-UP

Sixteen-year-old Steve Harmon is born and reared in Harlem. A student at Stuyvesant High School, he enjoys the film club and spends his spare time making films. He is roaming the neighborhood thinking about his next film when he is asked to be the lookout guy in a drugstore robbery. The only thing he has to do is to give a signal if the coast is clear. Then he is suddenly on trial for felony murder.

The novel, written as a film script and in journal entries, opens with Steve sitting in his cell at the Manhattan Detention Center thinking about all that has happened to him. He vividly reveals the culture of the detention center and describes his fears about violence and sexual assault. He tries to convince his readers that he isn't the monster that the attorneys call him. As he awaits his trial, he experiences self-doubt and begins to wonder if the attorneys are right about him.

Steve does well on the witness stand, and his film club advisor, George Sawicki, serves as a character witness. After a number of informants step up and tell the truth, James King is sentenced to prison for killing the store owner, and Steve Harmon is found not guilty and is released from jail.

When he returns home, he finds that his relationship with his father is strained, and his mother doesn't understand his obsession with a new film that he is making—one that examines who he really is.

Fans of the novel will want to read *Monster: A Graphic Novel*, adapted by Guy A. Sims and illustrated by Dawud Anyabwile (2015).

BEFORE READING

Ask your young reader to discuss the difference between an accomplice and an accessory. Find out which is more likely to receive a stricter charge by the courts. Brainstorm ways to avoid being used as an accomplice or an accessory in a crime.

SHARED DISCUSSION

- The novel opens with Steve Harmon sitting alone in his cell at the Manhattan Detention Center. Describe his thoughts and his fears. How do his fears escalate as his trial nears?

- Discuss what Steve should have done when he was asked to enter the drugstore and send a signal to James that the coast is clear. Steve isn't found guilty of murder, but he is an accomplice to the crime. Debate whether Steve should have served some prison time for his involvement.

- Discuss the structure of the novel. How are a movie script and journal entries effective ways of telling the story? Discuss how this style provides a more intimate and honest view of Steve's emotions. Explain why Steve titles his movie *Monster*. How does he try to convince himself that he isn't a monster?

- How does Miss O'Brien view Steve? Debate whether she believes he is guilty. Discuss her closing arguments in Steve's trial. Why do you think she gives Steve the cold shoulder after the jury declares him not guilty?

- Describe Steve's family. What is his mother's reaction when she sees her son in handcuffs? Discuss Steve's feelings after his parents have visited him in the detention center. Explain what Steve means when he says, "In a way I think she [mama] was mourning me as if I was dead." How does Steve's involvement in the crime change his relationship with his father?

- The novel has been challenged because of its violence. Debate why those who challenge the novel find it difficult to discuss issues related to violence. How might the novel serve as a cautionary tool for potential youth offenders? Explain how storytelling is an excellent way to make the young aware of societal issues related to incarcerated youth. How does storytelling build empathy toward those who are innocent?

- The profanity used in the book is another reason why it has been challenged. How does the language used in the novel reflect the prison culture? How does it reflect the street culture in Steve's neighborhood?

- There have also been censorship attempts related to issues of racism. Debate whether the attorneys in the novel are guilty of racial profiling. Identify other incidents of racism in the novel. What message is Myers communicating about race in America?

WRITING PROMPTS AND ACTIVITIES

- Mr. Sawicki, the film club mentor at Stuyvesant High School, says, "When you make a film, you leave an impression on the viewers, who serve as a kind of jury for your film." Write a journal entry that discusses the impression that Steve Harmon wants to leave on his viewers when he writes *Monster* from his jail cell.

- It is Miss O'Brien's job to make Steve seem different from Bobo, Osvaldo, and King in the eyes of the jury. Write an essay that discusses how Steve is different from these guys.

- The Universal Declaration of Human Rights, article 11, states that everyone is presumed innocent until proven guilty. Sponsor a debate that argues whether Steve Harmon is afforded this right in the novel. Specific scenes and direct quotes from the novel should be used to support the arguments.
- The novel ends five months after Steve's trial. He is making a movie about himself. Divide readers into groups and ask them to write a scene for the film where Steve talks about who he really is.
- Steve Harmon is only sixteen when he is acquitted of a felony murder charge. Find out what the Office of Juvenile Justice (https://ojjdp.ojp.gov/) is doing to help kids like Steve. Then identify local agencies that advocate for juvenile offenders.

READ-ALIKES

Liss, Steve, Marian Wright Edelman, and Cecilia Balli. *No Place for Children: Voices from Juvenile Detention*. 2005. 151 pp. University of Texas Press.

Ages 14-up. In the voices of kids held in juvenile detention centers in the United States, this work documents the horrific experiences of these incarcerated youth.

Marsden, John. *Letters from the Inside*. 1996. 160 pp. Laurel Leaf, an imprint of Penguin Random House.

Ages 12-up. This psychological drama tells the story of a friendship that develops between pen pals Tracey and Mandy, who meet through a newspaper advertisement for pen pals. They know little about one another, until it is revealed that Tracey is in juvenile detention and has lied about everything she put in her letters.

Myers, Walter Dean. *Lockdown*. 2010. 256 pp. HarperCollins.

Ages 14-up. Fourteen-year-old Reese is serving time in a juvenile correctional facility for stealing prescription pads and selling them to a drug dealer. He is trying to make the right choices so that he might earn an early release and a second chance on life.

Neri, G. Illus. by Randy DuBurke. *Yummy: The Last Days of a Southside Shorty*. 2010. 96 pp. Lee & Low.

Ages 12-up. This graphic novel is based on an actual event that occurred in 1994 on Chicago's South Side when eleven-year-old Robert "Yummy" Sandifer, a member of the Black Disciples gang, killed a fourteen-year-old girl. It is narrated by an eleven-year-old fictional character who knows Yummy and is attempting to understand his crime.

Watkins, Steve. *Juvie*. 2013. 320 pp. Candlewick.

Ages 14-up. Seventeen-year-old Sadie Windas, a good girl with a promising future, is caught up in a drug deal and is serving six months in a juvenile detention facility. The real issue is that Sadie confessed to the crime she didn't commit in an effort to keep her sister out of jail.

The Hate U Give

ANGIE THOMAS

To every kid in Georgetown and in all "the Gardens" of the world: your voices matter, your dreams matter, your lives matter. Be roses that grow in the concrete.

- HARPERCOLLINS 2018
- 512 PAGES
- AGES 14–UP

Sixteen-year-old Starr Carter is a Black girl who lives in the Garden Heights neighborhood of Harlem. She is caught between two worlds because she attends school at the exclusive Williamson Prep in Riverton Hills, where most of the students are white. She dates a white boy but is reluctant to introduce him to her father because she knows that he would disapprove.

During spring break, Starr attends a party at the home of Big D in her neighborhood and realizes just how different this world is from the one at school. Kenya, the girlfriend who invited her to the party, abandons her, causing Starr to feel lost and awkward. Then she sees Khalil Harris, her best friend from childhood. When they hear a shot fired, the two leave the party in Khalil's car. The real trouble begins when a cop pulls them over for an unknown reason. The cop forces Khalil out of the car and refuses to answer when Khalil asks him what they did wrong. Khalil looks in the window to ask Starr if she is okay, and the cop shoots him three times in the back. The unarmed teenager dies on the scene.

After Khalil is killed, memories of another senseless incident cause

Starr severe emotional distress. When she was in elementary school, a drive-by shooter killed her girlfriend as the two were playing on the sidewalk. Her white friends don't understand the world in which Starr lives, and her mother and Uncle Carlos, a policeman, believe the Carter family should leave Garden Heights. Maverick Carter, Starr's father and a former gang member who served time in prison, insists that they stay.

It takes a while for Starr to find her voice, but when the cop's father lies about the incident on television, she steps up to tell the truth about what happened to Khalil. She also implicates King, a local gang member and drug dealer. It turns out that Khalil was selling drugs to help support his family because his grandmother is in cancer treatment. Khalil wasn't a gang member, though King tries to claim that he was. When the grand jury issues a not guilty verdict in the cop's trial, the Garden Heights neighborhood erupts into violent demonstrations. There is looting, and Maverick Carter's store is burned down.

Maverick Carter intends to rebuild his store, and Starr plans to use her voice and speak out against racial injustices.

BEFORE READING

Ask your child to read about Black Lives Matter (https://blacklives matter.com/). What is the purpose of this global movement? How do they organize their work? Find out if there is a chapter in your community and what you can do to support their work.

SHARED DISCUSSION

- Describe Starr's family. Why does her father resent Uncle Carlos? Her mother wants to move the family out of the Garden Heights neighborhood. Why does Starr's father insist that they stay?
- Discuss the difference between racism and racial injustice. Starr

says, "It's dope to be black until it's hard to be black." Cite scenes in the novel where Starr finds it hard to be Black. How is she very aware of racism? She has good friends at Williamson Prep, but they don't understand the world in which she lives. Discuss the incident at school when Hailey makes an insensitive remark to Starr. What is zero tolerance? Do you think Starr is the victim of zero tolerance when she is suspended for punching Hailey?

- The grand jury finds the cop not guilty of the murder of Khalil. How is this an example of racial injustice? Discuss how Maverick explains racial injustice to Starr.

- Discuss Starr's reaction when she learns that Uncle Carlos has been placed on leave. How is he angry with himself for losing his temper? Explain what Uncle Carlos means when he says to Starr, "You're one reason I even became a cop, baby girl. Because I love you and all those folks in the neighborhood." What kind of difference does Uncle Carlos think he can make in the neighborhood? Suggest ways that communities can make their neighborhoods safe.

- What is the hope at the end of the novel? Compare Starr's vow to speak up about racial injustice to the Never Again movement that was formed after the mass shooting at Marjory Stoneman Douglas High School in Parkland, Florida. Why is it important to use your voice?

- The novel has been banned in schools because it is "pervasively vulgar." Define "vulgar" and discuss the scenes that some people call vulgar. Discuss whether these people judge scenes and words without looking at the entire book. Why is it important to think about the entire work and consider these scenes in context?

- The novel's depiction of racism is another reason why it has been challenged. Explain how the novel should be used to have important conversations about racism in our society.

- The most volatile challenges have come from policemen who call the book "almost an indoctrination of distrust of police." Discuss how police violence is a problem in the nation. How is this attempt to ban the book a denial of the existence of police violence?

WRITING PROMPTS AND ACTIVITIES

- Write an essay that explains the title of the novel.
- Khalil was selling drugs to support his family. Write a journal entry that discusses what Uncle Carlos means when he says, "He [Khalil] was more than any bad decision he made."
- Locate articles about the shooting death of Trayvon Martin. Write a journal entry that compares the killing of Khalil to that of Martin. How were both boys victims of racism and police brutality?
- In a note at the end of the paperback copy of the novel, Angie Thomas says, "Literature is a powerful thing." Write a journal entry that discusses the power of *The Hate U Give*. How is it both a mirror and a window to readers? Write a concluding paragraph that addresses how the novel spoke to you. How did it change your views about race and the criminal justice system in our nation?
- Read Jason Reynolds and Brendan Kiely's *All American Boys*, a novel where the main characters experience acts of police violence similar to the one Starr witnessed when her friend Khalil was murdered. Stage a talk show where Starr from *The Hate U Give* and Rashad and Quinn from *All American Boys* are guests. Have them discuss issues of police violence, their message to law enforcement, and their advice to young Americans about ways to effect change.

READ-ALIKES

Coles, Jay. *Tyler Johnson Was Here*. 2018. 304 pp. Little, Brown.
  Ages 14-up. Marvin, his twin brother Tyler, and their best friends are

leaving a convenience store when a police chase gives way to violence, and the police pull a gun on Marvin, an innocent bystander. Later the boys go to a party, the police are called to break up a commotion, and Tyler is gunned down by one of the officers.

Keplinger, Kody. *That's Not What Happened*. 2018. 326 pp. Scholastic.

Ages 14-up. Lee's best friend was killed in a high school massacre, and now she is faced with a hard decision: whether to speak up and tell the truth about what really happened or deal with the consequences of staying silent.

Lowery, Wesley. *They Can't Kill Us All: Ferguson, Baltimore, and a New Era in America's Racial Justice Movement*. 2016. 256 pp. Little, Brown.

Ages 14-up. In one of the first books on the Black Lives Matter movement, Lowery, the reporter that covered the murder of Michael Brown in Ferguson, Missouri, writes this work of nonfiction after being called upon to research and expose street violence in other cities.

Reynolds, Jason, and Brendan Kiely. *All American Boys*. 2015. 320 pp. Atheneum/Caitlyn Dlough, an imprint of Simon & Schuster.

Ages 14-up. Rashad, a Black teenager, is the victim of police brutality that lands him in the hospital with a broken nose and broken ribs. Quinn, a white teenager, witnessed the entire event and now must find the courage to speak up, even if it means losing a father figure— the white cop who committed the crime.

Watson, Renée. *Piecing Me Together*. 2017. 272 pp. Bloomsbury.

Ages 12-up. Jade is a scholarship student and one of the few African American students at Saint Francis High School, a prestigious school in Portland. She doesn't like the label "at risk," and after dealing with socioeconomic differences and racial inequality, she comes face-to-face with self-doubt.

PART III

REALITY AND TOUGH CHOICES

Children and teens deal with similar issues that have shaped the maturation process for generations, but today they face more complex matters related to their place in the world. Sometimes they must come to terms with family changes, grief, survival in an unstable environment, and issues related to sex, sexuality, and gender identity. They need books that mirror their world while at the same time offering them a glimpse into the lives of others. In this way, they develop empathy for those whose lives are different from theirs. These books give them the opportunity to think about real-life problems and concerns and see the possibility of hope in every situation.

Because of Winn-Dixie

KATE DICAMILLO

There ain't no way you can hold on to something that wants to go, you understand? You can only love what you got while you got it.

- 2001 NEWBERY HONOR
- CANDLEWICK 2001
- 192 PAGES
- AGES 9–12

Set in the small town of Naomi, Florida, ten-year-old India Opal Buloni and her father live in the adults-only Friendly Corners Trailer Park. Opal is allowed to live there because she is a quiet child and because her daddy is the preacher at Open Arms Baptist Church. One day the preacher sends Opal to pick up a few groceries, and she comes home with a stray dog that looks as lonely as Opal feels. She names him Winn-Dixie after the store where she found him. Opal doesn't have a friend in the world until Winn-Dixie comes into her life. She talks to him and tells him all about her life before moving to Naomi. She tells him how she misses her mama, who drank too much and left home because she wasn't very good at being a preacher's wife.

Winn-Dixie doesn't like to be left alone, so he and Opal are constant companions. Because of Winn-Dixie, Opal meets her first friend in Naomi, Miss Franny Block, the librarian at the Herman W. Block Memorial Library. Then Winn-Dixie leads Opal to Gloria Dump, a woman whom the mean Dewberry boys call a witch. It's Gloria Dump who introduces Opal to Littmus Lozenge, a mint that has a secret ingredient that tastes somewhat like sorrow. When Opal proposes that there be a party in Gloria's backyard, the older woman agrees, but with a stipulation: Opal must invite the Dewberry boys and pinched-faced Amanda Wilkinson. Opal invites the preacher; Miss Franny Block; Otis, a man from the pet store who spent time in jail because of his guitar playing; and kids from around town. The party is interrupted by a thunderstorm that causes Winn-Dixie to go into hiding. Opal and her father roam the town searching for him, and when they return to Gloria Dump's house, they find Winn-Dixie has been there all along—hiding under a bed. But it's at the party that Otis plays his guitar, and all the sadness and loneliness lift and friendships are formed.

Opal and the preacher discover a lot that night. The preacher tells Opal that he doesn't think her mother is ever coming back, but he also says, "Thank God your mama left me you."

BEFORE READING

Explain to your child that the main character of the novel is an only child and that she and her father have moved to a new town. Discuss the difference between being "alone" and being "lonely." What are ways a new kid in town might make friends?

SHARED DISCUSSION

- Explain why Opal calls her dad "the preacher." How does this help the reader understand their relationship? Debate how their relationship changes by the end of the novel. How is Winn-Dixie responsible for the changed relationship between Opal and her father?
- Opal says to Winn-Dixie, "You are a suffering dog, so maybe he [the preacher] will let me keep you." Discuss why Opal thinks that her dad will accept Winn-Dixie because he is suffering.

- Discuss the significance of the bottle tree in Gloria Dump's backyard. Why does she call it her "mistake tree"? How does the mistake tree help Opal come to terms with the fact that her mother isn't coming back?

- Gloria Dump introduces Opal to the Littmus Lozenge. What does the candy teach Opal about other suffering people in Naomi?

- What gives Opal the idea to have a party in Gloria Dump's backyard? Why does Gloria insist that Opal invite the Dewberry boys and Amanda Wilkinson?

- Adults have challenged the novel because of its profanity. Discuss the passage when Miss Franny Block says, "War is hell." Debate whether "hell" is profane language in this phrase. Why does Miss Franny think that "war should be a cuss word too"?

- Others have complained about the book because of alcoholism. Discuss how alcoholism is a very real issue in some families. How does Gloria Dump confront her alcoholism and begin her journey toward recovery?

- Some adults have issues with sad novels for young readers. How would you explain the hope beneath the sadness in the novel?

WRITING PROMPTS AND ACTIVITIES

- Opal has never seen her father cry until they are out looking for Winn-Dixie and her father wants to give up the search. Think about the conversation between father and daughter. Then write a journal entry that explains why the preacher cries.

- Write a character sketch of Gloria Dump. Explain her key role in resolving the conflict of the novel.

- Gloria Dump says to Opal, "Why don't you go and tell me everything about yourself, so as I can see you with my heart." Write a journal entry that discusses what Opal sees with her heart at the end of the novel. Cite specific passages from the novel to support your thoughts.

- Think about Winn-Dixie's role in helping Opal find friends. Then write an acrostic poem using "Winn-Dixie" as the spine word.
- At the beginning of the novel, Opal doesn't like the small town of Naomi, Florida. By the end of the novel, she has a different view of the town. Write a description of Naomi that Opal might write for the Chamber of Commerce to use with newcomers.

READ-ALIKES

Bundy, Tamara. *Walking with Miss Millie*. 2017. 227 pp. Nancy Paulsen Books, an imprint of Penguin Random House.

Ages 9–12. Alice is a newcomer in town, and she thinks the kids are bullies, and Clarence, the dog next door, is a beast. When she begins walking Clarence with his owner, Miss Millie, Alice shares her own story and discovers that the town is filled with kind people.

Corriveau, Art. *How I, Nicky Flynn, Finally Get a Life (And a Dog)*. 2010. 272 pp. Abrams.

Ages 9–12. Eleven-year-old Nicky is struggling with his parents' recent divorce, moving to a new town, and making new friends. When his mother brings home a guide dog that she rescued from the pound, Nicky runs away with the dog by his side. This stunt gains him much recognition from kids at school.

Lean, Sarah. *A Dog Called Homeless*. 2012. 208 pp. Katherine Tegen Books, an imprint of HarperCollins.

Ages 9–12. A year after her mother's death, fifth grader Cally Fisher sees her mother's ghost. Neither her father nor her older brother want to talk about it, but when the family moves, Cally meets a blind boy, a homeless man, and a silver-gray dog that teaches her the power of communication and how to share memories of her mother.

Martin, Ann M. *Everything for a Dog*. 2011. 240 pp. Square Fish, an imprint of Macmillan.

Ages 9–12. Henry puts a dog and everything for a dog on his Christmas list; Bone is a stray dog wanting a home; and Charlie is mourning the death of his older brother, but he finds some solace in his brother's dog. The three stories unite in the end just when each character needs joy returned to their life.

O'Connor, Barbara. *Wish*. 2016. 240 pp. Farrar, Straus & Giroux, an imprint of Macmillan.

Ages 9–12. Ten-year-old Charlie Reese goes to live with an aunt and uncle in the Blue Ridge Mountains of North Carolina after her father goes to jail and her mother becomes incapable of rearing her. She's angry and bitter, but when she finds Wishbone, a stray dog, she finally begins to see her situation in a different light.

Bridge to Terabithia

KATHERINE PATERSON

It was up to him to pay back to the world in beauty and caring what Leslie had loaned him in vision and strength.

- 1978 NEWBERY MEDAL
- HARPERCOLLINS 2017
- 191 PAGES
- AGES 9–12

Jess Aarons is striving to be the fastest runner in fifth grade at Lark Creek Elementary School. He won the race in fourth grade and became a hero for one day. Jess, an excellent artist, isn't considered a serious athlete; he is just a weird kid who can draw. But he has not forgotten the sweet taste of winning, and he aims to do it again. Then maybe his father will be proud of him.

The truth is that Jess's father, who works in DC, has little time to think about his son. He's simply interested in Jess's completing his chores on their farm in rural Virginia. Jess craves time to himself and wishes for a quiet place where he can draw and think. His father disapproves of his art, so Jess has no one with whom he can share his drawings except Miss Edmunds, his music teacher. Then, Leslie Burke comes into his life.

On the day of the race, Leslie, whose family has moved into the old Perkins place next to the Aarons' farm, enters the race and beats Jess right in front of all the guys. But something worth more than the championship happens that changes his life. He and Leslie become friends, and the two find a secret hiding place across the creek where they create an imaginary kingdom they call Terabithia. Their special place must be their secret because if others knew, the magic would be lost forever.

Some of the magic is lost for Jess when he returns from a museum trip and finds that Leslie has drowned trying to cross the log over the creek that leads to Terabithia. Jess makes a final trip to Terabithia alone. This time, he makes a wreath of wildflowers and places it on the "carpet of golden needles" in Leslie's memory. Then he builds a bridge to Terabithia and carefully leads May Belle, his little sister, across the bridge to the magical kingdom that Leslie helped to create, and he crowns her Queen of Terabithia. Leslie would be pleased.

BEFORE READING

Jess Aarons, the main character in *Bridge to Terabithia*, is an artist. He and Leslie, a friend who lives nearby, create an imaginary kingdom. Draw a picture of an imaginary kingdom where you and your best friend may go. Share the pictures with the group and talk about the special features of the kingdom that you created.

SHARED DISCUSSION

- Anger, hatred, sadness, love, pride, and jealousy are expressed in the novel. Discuss how Jess deals with each of these emotions.
- Why isn't Jess comfortable having Leslie at his house? Discuss whether he wants to keep their friendship private or whether his family embarrasses him. What are Mrs. Aarons's feelings about Leslie?
- Jess says that going to Terabithia without Leslie is no good. He needs her "to make the magic." What is magical about Leslie? How does Leslie change Jess?

- Discuss how Jess deals with his grief after Leslie dies. How does Leslie's death change Jess's relationship with his father? How does May Belle recognize Jess's grief?

- Leslie advises Jess about how to handle Janice Avery when she bullies him: "It's the *principle* of the thing, Jess. That's what you've got to understand. You have to stop people like that. Otherwise they turn into tyrants and dictators." Discuss Leslie's advice. Why is Janice Avery such a bully? Leslie says, "She deserves everything she gets and then some." Jess doesn't feel exactly the same way toward Janice. Why?

- The novel has been challenged and removed from the curriculum in schools throughout the United States because of "offensive language." Identify the offensive language. One phrase that has caused issues in schools is "Oh Lord." Some people feel this is taking the Lord's name in vain. How is the phrase part of the colloquialism of the region? What is a writer's responsibility to reflect a region as it is?

- Some censors feel that "the elaborate fantasy world might lead to confusion." How is fantasy a part of childhood? How might fantasy help a person deal with reality in the same way it helps Jess?

- People have objected to the novel because Leslie's family doesn't have a religion, and the Aarons only go to church on Easter. What is the difference between being religious and being spiritual? How is Leslie's family spiritual?

WRITING PROMPTS AND ACTIVITIES

- Jess says that he may one day write a letter to Mrs. Myers telling her that Leslie Burke thought she was a good teacher. Why does Jess think this might be important to Mrs. Myers? Write the letter that Jess wants to write.

- Terabithia is magical to Leslie and Jess, but Jess doesn't feel that he can draw Terabithia because he can't capture "the poetry of the trees." Leslie assures him, "You will someday." Draw a picture of Terabithia that Jess might draw when he does get "the poetry of the trees."

- Write a journal entry that explains the symbolism of the bridge that Jess builds for May Belle to cross over to the kingdom of Terabithia.

- What does Leslie mean when she says, "My parents are reassessing their value system"? What are their values? What would Mr. Aarons say his values are? Write a journal entry that contrasts the values of the Burkes and the Aarons. Use direct quotes and cite specific scenes from the novel to support your thoughts.

- Leslie is a good writer and loves language. Locate at least five poems that Leslie would find especially beautiful. Illustrate each poem and place them in a booklet for Jess.

READ-ALIKES

Goldblatt, Mark. *Finding the Worm*. 2016. 352 pp. Yearling, an imprint of Penguin Random House.

> Ages 9–12. Julian Twerski and the characters from *Twerp* are in the seventh grade and experiencing all the issues related to coming of age, but this time there is a much larger hurdle to cross—the untimely death of their friend Quentin from cancer.

Henkes, Kevin. *Olive's Ocean*. 2005. 224 pp. HarperCollins.

> Ages 9–12. In this 2004 Newbery Honor book, Olive Barstow is killed in a car accident, and her mother reveals a diary entry that stated Olive's strong desire to have Martha as a friend. She also dreamed of going to the ocean, so when Martha takes a vacation to Cape Cod, she realizes that she is there for both of them.

Park, Barbara. *Mick Harte Was Here.* **1996. 128 pp. Yearling, an imprint of Penguin Random House.**

Ages 9–12. Thirteen-year-old Phoebe Harte deals with the death of her younger brother by remembering the funny and sometimes annoying things that he used to do.

Shank, Marilyn Sue. *Child of the Mountains.* **2015. 272 pp. Yearling, an imprint of Penguin Random House.**

Ages 9–12. Set in 1953 in a small town in West Virginia, sixth grader Lydia Hawkins grieves for her grandmother and her little brother, B. J., who died of cystic fibrosis. She even grieves for her mother, who is sitting in jail for taking B. J. from the hospital so that he could die at home.

Spinelli, Jerry. *The Warden's Daughter.* **2017. 352 pp. Knopf, an imprint of Penguin Random House.**

Ages 9–12. Cammie O'Reilly's mother was killed when Cammie was a baby, so she has no parental guidance when her father is at work as the warden of Hancock County Prison. It's always been enough to spend her free time with the women prisoners in the exercise yard, but now that she is about to turn thirteen, she feels the loss of a mother in her life.

15 Melissa

ALEX GINO

She had genuinely started to believe that if people could see her onstage as Charlotte, maybe they would see that she was a girl offstage too.

- SCHOLASTIC 2022
- 208 PAGES
- ORIGINALLY PUBLISHED 2015 AS *GEORGE*
- AGES 8–12

Fourth grader George is transgender, but only she knows. When her teacher reads aloud *Charlotte's Web*, George sobs when Charlotte dies, causing the boys in her class to taunt and tease her. Then Ms. Udell tells the class that auditions will begin the following week for parts in the elementary school play based on E. B. White's novel. George really wants to play Charlotte and practices the role over the weekend. She's nervous about the auditions, but her best friend, Kelly, encourages her to try out for her dream role.

On the day of the auditions, Ms. Udell calls students one-by-one into the hall to audition for the play. George wants to audition for the role of Charlotte. Instead of taking her seriously, Ms. Udell tells George that she is "a fine young man" and should audition for the part of Wilbur or Templeton.

At home, George keeps a bag filled with girls' clothing and *Seventeen* magazines hidden in the back of her closet, and she calls herself Melissa. After school when she is home alone, George locks the door to her room and pulls out the bag. She later learns that Scott, her older brother, knows about the bag and thinks that George is gay. It's

Scott who teaches her how to erase the history on their mom's computer after George has searched information about being transgender.

Kelly, the student chosen to play Charlotte, is an independent thinker and launches a plan to help George realize her dream of playing Charlotte. Since there are two shows, Kelly will play the first show, and George the second one. They keep their plan a secret, and just before the curtain opens for the second show, George slips into the spider costume. She is an excellent actress and plays the role with compassion to an audience that appears confused. It appears that Mrs. Maldonado, the principal, had already realized George's identity struggle, and encourages George's mother to accept her child for who she is. At this point, things get better for George.

Kelly gives George some of her clothing and begins calling her Melissa, a sign of true acceptance.

BEFORE READING

Ask readers to define "transgender." Then have them discuss what the term "transitioning" means. Engage them in a discussion about the proper pronoun to use when referring to a transgender person. Transgender persons deserve safe spaces to be who they are. What is your role in helping them feel safe at school and within the community?

SHARED DISCUSSION

- Describe George and her relationship with Kelly. How does George know that she can trust Kelly with her secret? At first, Kelly is confused about George's identity. At what point does Kelly decide to support George and protect her against the class bullies?
- The boys in George's class bully her on the playground. They have no idea about George's identity, but they call her a "girl." Debate whether they think George is gay. Mrs. Udell reads aloud *Charlotte's*

Web, and George cries at the ending. How does Mrs. Udell handle George's emotions when the boys laugh at her?

- Discuss Mrs. Udell's reaction when George wants to play Charlotte in the fourth-grade play. How does it hurt George when Mrs. Udell calls her "a fine young man"?
- George is sent to the principal's office after she gets in a playground skirmish with Jeff. George sees a sign in Mrs. Maldonado's office that says, "Support Safe Spaces for Gay, Lesbian, Bisexual, and Transgender Youth." How does this cause George to wonder where her safe space is?
- At what point does George's mother express concern about George's sexual identity? Why does she think George is gay? How is she confused by George's gender identity? Discuss how George's mother reacts after George's successful performance as Charlotte.
- *Melissa* has been challenged because it's about a transgender character. Discuss why it's important for the young to read about transgender youth. How might the novel help students be more compassionate toward those transitioning and those who have already transitioned? How might knowledge and compassion eliminate bullying?
- The novel has also been challenged because Scott, George's brother, teaches her how to erase the history on her mother's computer. Discuss how this explains George's need for privacy. What does this scene reveal about Scott and his understanding of George's true identity?
- There have also been adults who have challenged the book because there is a reference to "dirty magazines." Discuss why Scott believes that looking at dirty magazines is a sign of growing up. Explain why adults who are upset with this reference may actually be in denial about the process of growing up.

WRITING PROMPTS AND ACTIVITIES

- George says, "Being a secret girl was a giant problem." Document the problems that George experiences. Write a brief journal entry that explains whether George's problems improve once she reveals her identity.

- Write an article for the local newspaper about George's performance as Charlotte in the fourth-grade play. Include a quote from Kelly, Ms. Udell, Mrs. Maldonado, and George's mother.

- Read the interview with Alex Gino at the end of the paperback book. Then write a brief journal entry that draws a comparison between Melissa and Gino's life.

- Explain what Gino means when they express hope that one day *Melissa* might be labeled historical fiction. Put yourself in the future and write an entry about *Melissa* for a book on historical children's literature.

- Consider the sign that George sees in Mrs. Maldonado's office about safe spaces. Debate whether safe spaces can exist without understanding and communication. Allow readers to work in groups to make a plan for creating a safe space for students like Melissa.

READ-ALIKES

Clarke, Cat. *The Pants Project*. 2017. 272 pp. Sourcebooks Jabberwocky, an imprint of Sourcebooks, Inc.

Ages 9–12. Sixth grader Liv, born Olivia, appears as a girl to classmates, but he is truly and secretly a boy. Encouraged by his two moms, Liv lodges a protest against the middle school dress code that requires girls to wear skirts. There are bullies and lost friendships, but in the end he is triumphant.

Gephart, Donna. *Lily and Dunkin*. 2016. 352 pp. Delacorte, an imprint of Penguin Random House.

Ages 12-up. Eighth grader Lily McGrother, born Timothy McGrother, is accepted at home, but revealing her secret at school is another matter. When she meets a new boy who harbors a different kind of secret, the two create an unique bond as they deal with bullies and their own realities.

Hennessey, M. G. *The Other Boy*. 2016. 228 pp. HarperCollins.

Ages 8–12. Twelve-year-old Shane is a typical boy to his classmates, but to his divorced parents he is the source of conflict because his mother favors the hormone blockers that Shane takes to prevent female puberty, and his father is against it. Shane, an artist, works diligently on a graphic novel as he struggles to calm his fears that his friends might discover his secret.

Jennings, Jazz. *Being Jazz: My Life as a (Transgender) Teen*. 2016. 272 pp. Crown Books for Young Readers, an imprint of Penguin Random House.

Ages 12-up. This true story of Jazz Jennings, the star of the popular TLC show *I Am Jazz,* chronicles her life beginning at age five when she began transitioning to a girl.

Polonsky, Ami. *Gracefully Grayson*. 2016. 250 pp. Hyperion.

Ages 10-up. Sixth grader Grayson is secretly a girl, but she worries about revealing herself to family and friends. When she is cast as Persephone in the Porter Middle School spring play, she gains courage, with the help of a few new friends, to unveil her true identity.

The Higher Power of Lucky

SUSAN PATRON

Some aspects of life are strange or even terrible, but later something okay or even good happens that would never have happened without the bad/strange thing. 2007 Newbery Medal

- SIMON & SCHUSTER 2006
- 194 PAGES
- AGES 9–12

Set in the desert town of Hard Pan, California (population forty-three), the only thing wrong with ten-year-old Lucky Trimble's life is that she doesn't have an actual mother. Instead she has Brigitte, her father's ex-wife and her legal guardian, who has come all the way from France to care for her. The two occupy a little trailer that is comfortable but not very private.

The center of Hard Pan is the Found Object Wind Chime Museum. One day Lucky is cleaning up around the museum and overhears Short Sammy through the fence say that his dog got "bitten on the scrotum" by a rattlesnake. Lucky doesn't know what the word "scrotum" means, but at the end of the novel she finally asks. The museum also hosts the anonymous twelve-step meetings—alcoholics, gamblers, smokers, and overeaters. Lucky overhears Short Sammy talk about his "rock-bottom" moment with alcohol and how he finds his "Higher Power," but she doesn't understand how one actually finds it.

In addition to her work at the museum, Lucky enjoys hanging out with five-year-old Miles, who lives with his grandmother while his mother serves a prison term, and Lincoln, a knot-tying champion whose mother wants him to one day be president. They are the only kids in town.

When Lucky overhears Brigitte's telephone conversations with her mother back in France, she becomes concerned that Brigitte is home-sick. Her suspicions grow when she sees Brigitte's passport and legal documents spread out in full view. At this point, Lucky feels that the only way to avoid being placed with a foster family is to run away. She packs a survival kit and takes off. Things don't go exactly as planned because Lincoln and Miles, the entire town, and one almost actual mother lead her home. Lucky's journey continues in *Lucky Breaks* (2009) and *Lucky for Good* (2011).

BEFORE READING

Tell readers that the novel is set in a desert town with a population of forty-three. There are only three kids who live there. Ask them to discuss the advantages and disadvantages of living in such a small place. Describe a possible day in the life of the three kids who live in Hard Pan.

SHARED DISCUSSION

- Lucky, Lincoln, and Miles are the only kids in Hard Pan. Describe their relationship. Miles is especially annoying to Lucky. Debate whether it's his age, his personality, or the echo of him in Lucky's own longing for a mom that sometimes irritates her.
- Abandonment is a central theme in *The Higher Power of Lucky*. How does Lucky deal with the death of her mother and the fact that her father doesn't want her? Debate whether Brigitte's decision to adopt her changes Lucky's feelings of abandonment. Miles's mother is in jail. Why does he think his situation is better than Lucky's?

- Lucky's father asked Brigitte to take care of Lucky until she could be placed in a foster home. Brigitte says that she would want a foster home that would give Lucky a little freedom but some discipline as well. Discuss whether Brigitte offers this type of home environment for Lucky.
- Lucky eavesdrops at the anonymous twelve-step meetings at the museum and learns that each person is in search of a Higher Power. Discuss why Lucky is so eager to find her Higher Power.
- The twelve-step people talk about rock-bottom moments before finding their Higher Power. What is Lucky's rock-bottom moment? Explain why the "getting in control of your life" step is especially difficult for Lucky.
- When the novel won the Newbery Medal, newspapers and talk radio shows across the nation raised questions about the book because Lucky hears Short Sammy say that his dog was bitten on the "scrotum" by a rattlesnake. Discuss why some adults don't think it's appropriate for children to read about parts of the anatomy. Why is it better to use the proper word, rather than a slang term?
- Why is it wrong to take words out of context? How does this promote censorship?
- At the end of the novel, Lucky asks Brigitte, "What is a scrotum?" How does this question bring the novel full circle?

WRITING PROMPTS AND ACTIVITIES

- Write an essay that discusses the point in the novel when Lucky discovers her Higher Power. Include a concluding paragraph that reveals how discovering her Higher Power sets her life on a different course.
- Symbolism is the representation of an idea or an object by something else. Write a paragraph that explains the symbolism of Lucky plugging up the knothole in the fence of the museum.

- Lucky thinks that Lincoln is grave, serious, and diplomatic, the qualities of a future president. Write a character sketch of Lincoln that reveals his grave, serious, and diplomatic nature. Use direct quotes or scenes from the novel to support your thoughts.
- Write a description of Hard Pan for a book about California. Include information about daily life, places to eat, sights, and the people.
- Write a letter to an adult who may be troubled by the word "scrotum," and explain to them why it is an appropriate word to use in the book. Include a statement about the symbolism of Lucky's question at the end of the novel.

READ-ALIKES

Giff, Patricia Reilly. *Pictures of Hollis Woods*. 2002. 176 pp. Wendy Lamb Books, an imprint of Penguin Random House.

Ages 10–12. Hollis Woods was abandoned as a baby and has run away from several foster homes. Things get better when she goes to live with Josie, an artist who appreciates Hollis's creativity, but then Josie begins slipping away into dementia, and Hollis knows it's up to her to save Josie and herself. A 2003 Newbery Honor book.

Naylor, Phyllis Reynolds. *The Agony of Alice*. 2011. 176 pp. Simon & Schuster.

Ages 9–12. Alice McKinley's mother died when she was younger, and now that she is entering sixth grade, she wants a woman in her life who can guide her. Her father and older brother are loving and attentive, but they just don't understand girl issues.

Paterson, Katherine. *The Great Gilly Hopkins*. 2004. 192 pp. HarperCollins.

Ages 9–12. In this 1979 Newbery Honor book, eleven-year-old Gilly is labeled "hard to manage" after stints in two different foster homes. When she is placed with Mrs. Trotter, a tough but caring semiliterate foster mother, Gilly begins to understand life and the meaning of love.

Shofner, Corabel. *Almost Paradise*. 2017. 204 pp. Farrar, Straus & Giroux, an imprint of Macmillan.

Ages 9–12. Ruby Clyde Henderson is twelve years old when her mother goes to jail for being an accomplice to robbing a convenience store. Ruby makes her way to Cypress Mill, Texas, where her mother's identical twin, Sister Eleanor, lives as a solitary Episcopal nun.

Uss, Christina. *The Adventures of a Girl Called Bicycle*. 2019. 320 pp. Margaret Ferguson Books, an imprint of Holiday House.

Ages 9–12. This clever and witty novel stars twelve-year-old Bicycle, who was only a toddler when she was left on the steps of the Mostly Silent Monastery to be reared by the monks, and Sister Wanda, who decides that what Bicycle needs most are friends her own age.

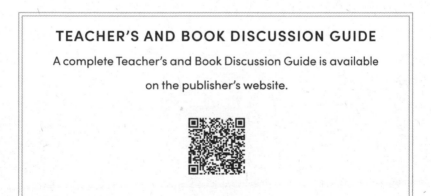

TEACHER'S AND BOOK DISCUSSION GUIDE

A complete Teacher's and Book Discussion Guide is available on the publisher's website.

17

Shiloh

PHYLLIS REYNOLDS NAYLOR

If Jesus ever comes back to earth again, I'm thinking, he'll come as a dog, because there isn't anything as humble or patient or loving or loyal as the dog I have in my arms right now.

- 1992 NEWBERY MEDAL
- ATHENEUM, AN IMPRINT OF SIMON & SCHUSTER 1991
- 144 PAGES
- AGES 9–12

Eleven-year-old Marty Preston lives with his parents and two younger sisters in the small Appalachian town of Friendly, West Virginia. One day Marty is walking down the winding road near the old Shiloh schoolhouse when he spots a small beagle. The dog looks hungry and shows signs of physical abuse. Marty's father thinks the dog belongs to Judd Travers, a man who is noted for abusing his dogs.

In Appalachia, people mind their own business, and Marty's father tells him that he must return the dog to Judd. Marty has always been obedient, and he and his father go to Judd's run-down trailer where Marty witnesses Judd, a drinking man, kick his dogs and shout profanities at them. Judd doesn't even name his dogs. He simply calls them "one, two, three dammit." It pains Marty to leave the dog behind, but he reluctantly climbs into his father's vehicle and returns home with a heavy heart.

Not too long later, Shiloh reappears at the Preston home, and Marty is faced with a moral dilemma. He can lie to his parents and hide Shiloh in a makeshift pen on the back part of their property, or he can allow Shiloh to be a victim of Judd's abuse. He decides to keep the beagle and saves food from his own dinner to feed him. Then another dog attacks Shiloh, and Marty's secret is revealed.

Marty and his dad take Shiloh to Doc Murphy to be mended, but Marty is once again told that he must return the dog to Judd Travers. This time Marty blackmails Judd into selling him Shiloh after he witnesses Judd shooting deer out of season. Though a deal is cut, Judd isn't a man of his word, and Marty has to come up with other ideas for saving the dog.

Marty's encounter with Judd Travers and his fight to keep Shiloh continues in *Shiloh Season* (1996), *Saving Shiloh* (1997), and *A Shiloh Christmas* (2015).

BEFORE READING

Ask readers to discuss the meaning of a moral dilemma. Encourage readers to share real-life examples of a moral dilemma. Debate whether lying to save an abused animal is a moral dilemma.

SHARED DISCUSSION

- Marty loves animals. What details does Naylor provide right from the opening paragraphs that make this clear to readers?
- Marty feels that his choices come down to either hiding the dog he calls Shiloh or giving him back to Judd Travers. Debate whether there are other possibilities that Marty hasn't considered.
- "Thought once if I could just get Shiloh for my own, it would be the finest day of my life," Marty says, after he and Shiloh's original owner, Judd Travers, reach their agreement. "In a way it is, in a way it isn't." Why is Marty so torn?
- Marty's best friend is David Howard, the only child of two professional parents. Compare and contrast David's home with Marty's. What are some of the material advantages that the

Howards enjoy? How comfortable is David at Marty's home? What draws the boys to each other?

- Cite evidence that religion is important to the Preston family. How does Marty call upon his religious training when he is sorting out the lies that he tells?

- Parents have challenged the novel because Marty doesn't use proper English. Explain how Marty's Appalachian dialect is viewed as poor grammar. How does his use of language help define the setting?

- The novel has also been challenged because Marty lies to his parents about Shiloh. Marty's father says the dog belongs to Judd Travers and must be returned even if the dog is abused. How does Marty's desire to protect Shiloh cause him to lie to his parents? Explain how this is a moral dilemma for Marty.

- There have been challenges to the novel because Judd abuses alcohol and his dogs. Discuss how Judd is the villain in the novel. How would you explain to those who are offended by Judd's character that he isn't the character to be admired?

WRITING PROMPTS AND ACTIVITIES

- In Appalachia where *Shiloh* is set, there is a relationship between the land and the people. In small groups, discuss how the land shapes the people. How do the people shape the land? Write a brochure for the Tyler County Welcome Center that explains this to outsiders who want to better understand the area and its people. Include a map of Tyler County and pictures clipped from sites on the internet.

- Judd Travers violates hunting laws. Write a journal entry that discusses how his illegal actions are so dangerous to the community at-large.

- Marty experiences various emotions in the novel. For example, he feels anger, fear, happiness, and sadness. Write an essay that reveals these emotions in Marty. Cite specific scenes in the novel and use direct quotes to support your thoughts.

- Write a brief journal entry that explains what Marty means when he says, "You can lie not only by what you say but what you don't say." Cite specific scenes where Marty tells a lie and lies by not saying anything.

- Write a journal entry that discusses the "evil" sides of Judd Travers. Include a concluding paragraph that reveals Marty's view of Judd at the end of the novel.

READ-ALIKES

Appelt, Kathi. *The Underneath*. 2008. 320 pp. Atheneum, an imprint of Simon & Schuster.

Ages 9–12. Gar Face, a cruel trapper, chains his hound Ranger and abuses a mother cat and her kittens until the three animals find a way to survive together.

Kadohata, Cynthia. *Cracker! The Best Dog in Vietnam*. 2007. 320 pp. Atheneum, an imprint of Simon & Schuster.

Ages 10–14. Rick Hanski is only seventeen when he is sent to Vietnam and paired with a German shepherd that is trained to sniff bombs. The two must learn to be friends and trust each other if they are to survive.

London, Jack. *White Fang*. (originally published in 1906) 1989. 272 pp. Tor/ Forge.

Ages 10–14. Set during the Klondike gold rush, White Fang, a wolf dog, experiences cruelty from animals and humans before he finally meets human kindness.

O'Connor, Barbara. *How to Steal a Dog*. 2009. 192 pp. Square Fish, an imprint of Macmillan.

Ages 9–12. Georgina and her family are down and out, so she launches a plan to steal a dog and collect reward money. The problem is that she doesn't count on her conscience causing her to think about right and wrong.

Salisbury, Graham. *Banjo*. **2019. 212 pp. Wendy Lamb Books, an imprint of Penguin Random House.**

Ages 9–12. When a neighbor accuses Danny Mack's dog, Banjo, of chasing his sheep, the sheriff is called, and Danny's father insists that they must follow the law and put the dog down. Danny manages to save the dog's life, but he lies to his father that he had followed his orders.

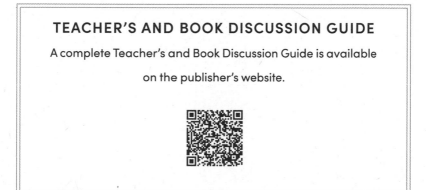

TEACHER'S AND BOOK DISCUSSION GUIDE

A complete Teacher's and Book Discussion Guide is available on the publisher's website.

18

Walk Two Moons

SHARON CREECH

A person had to go out and do things and see
things, and I wondered, for the first time, if this had
something to do with Gram and Gramps taking me on
this trip.

- 1995 NEWBERY MEDAL
- HARPERCOLLINS 1994
- 288 PAGES
- AGES 9–12

Thirteen-year-old Salamanca Tree Hiddle, Sal for short, embarks on a journey from Euclid, Ohio, to Lewiston, Idaho, with her grandparents in search of her mother. One day her mother, Chanhassen "Sugar" Pickford Hiddle, had simply left on a bus and headed west. Sal cannot grasp the grief that her mother felt upon delivering a stillborn child and instead feels that she may be the cause of her mother's leaving home. She follows her mother's travels through postcards that Sugar sends. Now Sal is seeing the same sites. As the travelers make their way west, Sal tells her grandparents the story of Phoebe Winterbottom and her mother's disappearance.

Sal's father wants a new life, so he moves them from their farm in Bybanks, Kentucky, to Euclid, Ohio, where Margaret Cadaver lives. Sal is angry about the move and doesn't recognize that her father is hurting and needs to move on with his life. What she doesn't know is why her father had gone to Lewiston, Idaho, and why he didn't take her with him. What she is certain about is that she doesn't like Margaret Cadaver and that her father had formed a relationship with Margaret when he went to Idaho. But she does like Phoebe Winterbottom, one of the first people she meets in Euclid.

Sal and Phoebe bond when they discover that they have something in common. Phoebe arrives home from school one day and discovers that her mother has left. There are mysteries to uncover when strange messages begin appearing on the doorsteps of the Winterbottom home. Sal and Phoebe are convinced these notes are from a "lunatic." And they believe that person is the young man who came to the door asking for Mrs. Winterbottom. His true identity is later revealed when Mrs. Winterbottom returns home.

When Sal and her grandparents reach Idaho, she learns that her mother was killed in a bus accident. It turns out that Sal's father knew her mother was dead and had gone to Idaho to bury her high on a hill overlooking the river. He didn't tell Sal that her mother was dead because he felt that by tracing her mother's journey she would come to terms with her death.

As Sal deals with her mother's death, Gram becomes sick and ultimately dies. They bury her on the farm in Kentucky. Sal and her father move back to the farm where they and Gramps once again find joy in their lives. They are even preparing for their friends in Ohio to visit.

BEFORE READING

Ask the group to interpret the following quote: "Don't judge a man until you've walked two moons in his moccasins." Then consider the title of the book and discuss the possible conflict. How does the title imply a journey?

SHARED DISCUSSION

- Discuss the purpose of Sal's trip with her grandparents. Explain what Sal means when she says, "It was not a trip that I was eager to take, but it was one I had to take." What does Sal learn on her journey? Why does Sal say that she didn't think she would survive the trip?

- Explain the parallel stories in the novel. What do Sal and Phoebe have in common? How does relating Phoebe's story to her grandparents help Sal come to terms with her own loss? Discuss why Gram feels sorry for Mrs. Winterbottom. Why does Mrs. Winterbottom leave her family? Explain Sal's feelings of jealousy toward Phoebe when Mrs. Winterbottom comes home at the end of the novel.

- Discuss the role of the lunatic in the disappearance of Sal's mother. Why does Sal think that it is her fault that her mother left? How does Sal react when she learns the true identity of the lunatic?

- Sal is the protagonist of the novel. Who is the antagonist? Explain Sal's reaction to her. How does the antagonist connect the story at the end?

- Discuss how Creech uses the literary elements of flashback and foreshadowing to relate Sal's story. Cite examples from the book.

- The book has been challenged for its "sexual content." What scenes are they referencing? How is Sal surprised when Ben kisses her? Discuss how this is a normal adolescent behavior. Gramps makes reference to the "marriage bed." Make a case that kissing and simply mentioning the "marriage bed" aren't sexual content.

- Others have challenged the novel because they feel it is too sad for young readers. While the novel is sad, the story is really about Sal's journey. Why is it important for readers to understand the sadness that many families face? Explain why it is equally important for readers to understand the journey toward healing. How does Creech end the novel with hope?

- The novel has also been challenged because of the way Native Americans are portrayed. Sal's mother is from the Seneca tribe. Cite references from the novel that reveal Sal's mother's ancestry. Debate the argument of critics that these passages are stereotypical images and therefore offensive. Take another look at the chapter where Sal and her grandparents visit the Wisconsin Dells and Gram joins the Native Americans in dancing. Discuss whether the purpose of this performance by the Native Americans is to entertain the tourists. If so, how might this scene be viewed differently?

WRITING PROMPTS AND ACTIVITIES

- Loss is a central theme in the book. Other than Sal, which other characters deal with loss? Select one character from the novel and write a journal entry that discusses their loss and personal journey. Cite passages from the story and use direct quotes to support your thoughts.

- A symbol is a person, place, or object that stands for something else. It is a literary element that helps readers connect to the overall meaning of a work. Blackberries and Sugar Hiddle and Norma Winterbottom cutting off their hair before they leave home are symbols in the novel. How do these symbols contribute to the readers, understanding of the story? Have readers select one of these symbols and write a brief journal entry that explains its meaning. Cite specific scenes and use direct quotes to support your thoughts.

- Sal and her father move back to their farm in Kentucky. Write a letter that Sal may write to Phoebe that expresses how life back on her beloved farm brings her journey full circle.

- In an interview, Sharon Creech says that the book doesn't have one message. She believes each reader may find different messages. Write a journal entry that conveys the message you glean from the novel.

- The lunatic leaves four messages on the doorsteps of the Winterbottom home. The first message left is the one used in the Before Reading activity. The additional messages are the following:
  - ► "Everyone has his own agenda."
  - ► "In the course of a lifetime, what does it matter?"
  - ► "You can't keep the birds of sadness from flying over your head, but you can keep them from nesting in your hair."
- Write a brief journal entry that discusses the meaning of one of these messages and how the message gives meaning to Sal's journey. Cite specific passages from the novel to support your thoughts.

READ-ALIKES

Creech, Sharon. *Ruby Holler*. 2012. 288 pp. HarperCollins.

Ages 9–12. Orphaned twins Dallas and Florida have been trouble in each foster home where they've lived, but when they are placed with Tiller and Sairy Morey in rural Ruby Holler, the duo find unexpected adventures and, ultimately, they discover home.

Hicks, Faith Erin. *Friends with Boys*. 2012. 224 pp. First Second Books, an imprint of Macmillan.

Ages 12-up. In this graphic novel, Maggie McKay finds herself in new territory when she enters high school after being homeschooled and at the same time deals with why her mother abandoned her family. A ghost appears throughout the story to help Maggie get over each hurdle.

Moranville, Sharelle Byars. *27 Magic Words*. 2016. 208 pp. Holiday House.

Ages 9–12. After ten-year-old Kobi's parents disappeared at sea when she was five, she used a magic word to bring up an image of them. As she tries to fit in at school, she tells outlandish stories about the whereabouts of her parents, but when the magic word and her lies begin to fail her, she must confront the truth before she can move on with her life.

Selznick, Brian. *Wonderstruck*. 2011. 640 pp. Scholastic.

> Ages 10–up. With over 460 illustrations, these parallel stories set in different eras connect as Ben, who is dealing with the death of his mother and wonders about his father, and Rose, a deaf girl who dreams of a mysterious actress, run away to New York City in search of the parts of their lives that are missing.

Sloan, Holly Goldberg. *Counting by 7s*. 2013. 384 pp. Dial, an imprint of Penguin Random House.

> Ages 9–12. Twelve-year-old Willow Chance has unusual behaviors, but when she enters middle school, she discovers a multicultural group of friends who teach her about belonging and family after her adopted parents are killed in a car accident.

19

Speak

LAURIE HALSE ANDERSON

Somebody slams into my chest and knocks me back into the closet. The light flicks on and the door closes. I'm trapped with Andy Evans.

- 2000 MICHAEL L. PRINTZ HONOR
- FARRAR, STRAUS & GIROUX, AN IMPRINT OF MACMILLAN 1999
- 208 PAGES
- AGES 14-UP

Melinda Sordino is looking forward to her freshman year at Merryweather High School. In middle school, she belonged to a group of friends, a gang that called themselves the Plain Janes. Everything changes in one night when Melinda and her friends attend a party where there are upperclassmen and a lot of underage drinking.

Andy Evans is one of the older kids at the party. He is extremely popular, and every girl's heartthrob. He approaches Melinda and takes her to the nearby woods and rapes her. She calls the cops, but before they arrive, she becomes frightened and takes off for home. Everyone at the party blames Melinda for reporting them to the cops, but they don't know the real story.

She is shunned by the Plain Janes and begins her ninth-grade year without a single friend. She lapses into a deep depression and is unable to speak. Her grades suffer, and she skips a lot of school. Her parents, who aren't good at communicating with one another or with Melinda, don't realize their daughter's troubles. Her teachers, except for her art teacher, refuse to believe that anything is going on with a seemingly apathetic student.

Melinda finally gains the courage to tell David Petrakis, her lab partner, about what happened to her last summer. He encourages her to speak up. Andy Evans asks Rachel, Melinda's former best friend, to the prom. When Melinda attempts to tell Rachel what happened at the party, Rachel refuses to believe that Andy would commit such a violent act. Then he gets physical with Rachel, and she dumps him before their prom date. Andy becomes so angry that he pushes Melinda into a janitor's closet and locks the door. She manages to escape, confides in her art teacher, and finally regains her friends.

Speak: The Graphic Novel (2018) is illustrated by Emily Carroll, and *Shout* (2019), a memoir written in free verse, details Anderson's own experience at the hand of a rapist.

BEFORE READING

Introduce the novel by telling readers that it's the story of a high school freshman who is raped when she attends a party where there is underage drinking. Consider the title of the novel and write a paragraph that suggests the internal conflict of the protagonist. Allow time for readers to read aloud their paragraphs.

SHARED DISCUSSION

- Describe Merryweather High School. The school had been known as the Trojans for years. Explain why the administration wants to change the mascot. Why are they having a tough time naming an "appropriate" mascot? What message are they sending the student body in their effort to make this change?
- Discuss the cliques at Merryweather High School. Melinda doesn't belong to a group, but things change for her after students find out what happened to her at the party. Debate whether Melinda would be interested in joining a group for her sophomore year.

- Melinda's friends, especially Rachel, betray her. Melinda says, "If there is anyone in the entire galaxy I am dying to tell what really happened, it's Rachel." Why doesn't she tell Rachael? What does it take for Rachael to realize what happened to Melinda?

- Melinda becomes silent after Andy rapes her at the party. Why is she afraid of speaking? Explain how David Petrakis helps her find her voice. What gives her the courage to tell her art teacher what happened to her?

- Melinda refers to Andy as "It." Explain why she can't bring herself to say his name. Andy slams Melinda into a closet at school because she told Rachael what had happened at the party. Explain how the other students at Merryweather react when they find out what Andy Evans did to Melinda.

- The novel has been challenged because of its depiction of a rape. Explain why some adults refuse to admit the rape culture in schools. How has the Me Too Movement brought these issues front and center?

- Others have challenged the book because of its depiction of underage drinking. How is underage drinking a very real problem in high schools? Explain why peer pressure makes teenagers engage in such activities. Discuss what you should do if you find yourself in a similar situation.

- Describe Melinda's family. Why doesn't she tell them what happened to her at the party? Explain why communication with family is so important in dealing with acts of sexual violence, underage drinking, and other challenges that teens face.

WRITING PROMPTS AND ACTIVITIES

- Write an essay that interprets the following quote: "The time has come to arm-wrestle some demons." What are Melinda's demons?

How does she eventually wrestle them? Write a concluding paragraph that expresses how Melinda wins the fight.

- When *Speak* was challenged in Missouri, Anderson's publisher took out a full-page ad in the *New York Times* that simply said, "Speak Loudly." Write an essay called "Speak Loudly" that discusses why it's important for people to report sex abuse.
- Mr. Freeman, the art teacher, gives students a blank sheet of paper and challenges the students to "make an object say something" by the end of the year. Think about Melinda's object, which becomes the cover of the book. What does it say? How does it reveal Melinda's journey?
- April is National Sexual Assault Awareness Month. The Rape, Abuse & Incest National Network (RAINN) supports survivors of sexual abuse. Find out which local organizations belong to RAINN. What services do they provide victims? How are they funded? What laws in your state support and protect survivors?
- Prepare a speech that Melinda might deliver at a rape victim support group. In the speech, trace Melinda's journey from victim to survivor.

READ-ALIKES

Downham, Jenny. *You Against Me*. 2012. 416 pp. Ember, an imprint of Penguin Random House.

> Ages 14–up. When Mikey's sister, Karyn, is raped by Tom Parker, Mikey sets out to seek revenge for his sister. Then he meets Tom's sister, the only witness to the crime, and he finds himself in an awkward situation when he falls for her.

Levine, Ellen. *In Trouble*. 2011. 208 pp. Lerner.

> Ages 14–up. Two best friends are juniors in high school when they each discover they are pregnant. Jamie is raped, but Elaine is pregnant by her boyfriend. Set in the 1950s, each girl must weigh their options against the social mores of the 1950s.

Marcus, Kimberly. *Exposed*. **2012. 272 pp. Ember, an imprint of Penguin Random House.**

Ages 14–up. Liz and Kate are best friends, but when Liz's brother rapes Kate, their friendship falls apart. Written in free verse from Liz's point of view, both girls must deal with the harsh realities of sexual violence and how it changes lives.

Ostrom, Melissa. *Unleaving*. **2019. 291 pp. Feiwel & Friends, an imprint of Macmillan.**

Ages 14–up. Nineteen-year-old Maggie is the victim of an assault at an off-campus party, and as she struggles to forget the brutal details of the violent act, she elects to live in an isolated cabin that belongs to an aunt. After she reports the crime, several popular athletes are expelled.

Smith, Amber. *The Way I Used to Be*. **2016. 384 pp. Margaret K. McElderry Books, an imprint of Simon & Schuster.**

Ages 14–up. Told in four parts, one for each year in high school. Eden McCrorey was a good student and had friends until her brother's best friend raped her in her own bed when she was a freshman in high school. Then things fall apart.

The Contender

ROBERT LIPSYTE

It's the climbing that makes the man. Getting to the top is an extra reward.

- HARPERCOLLINS REISSUE 2018
- 240 PAGES
- AGES 12–UP

Seventeen-year-old Alfred Brooks lives with his widowed Aunt Pearl and her three daughters in a small apartment in the heart of Harlem. Alfred, a high school dropout, tries to live a straight life and avoid the bad influences of his ghetto environment by taking a job at the Epsteins' grocery store. James, Alfred's best friend, is hooked on drugs and will do anything to support his habit. When Alfred accidentally mentions that the Epsteins leave money in the cash register on Friday nights, James and his gang decide to rob the store to get quick cash. James is arrested, and Alfred is faced with the guilt that he didn't warn his friend about the store's burglar alarm. But, more importantly, he worries that the Epsteins will no longer trust him.

Trying to deal with his guilt and avoid the gang, Alfred wanders the Harlem streets and happens upon Donatelli's Gym. The faint memory of his father telling him about the boxers such as Joe Louis and Sugar Ray Robinson who worked out there helps Alfred to realize, "They weren't no slave, and they didn't have to bust into anybody's grocery store. They made it. They got to be somebody."

In what turns out to be a symbolic climb, Alfred ascends the stairs to the gym and commits himself to being a "contender." While Alfred eventually learns that he doesn't have the "killer instinct" to make it as a boxer, his training helps him gain control of his life. Meanwhile, Alfred never gives up on James. When James escapes, badly cut, after a second attempt to break into the Epsteins' store, Alfred searches for him and finds him in a Central Park cave, their childhood hideout. Alfred offers to help set James straight and reconfirms his support and friendship by giving his bleeding friend his blood.

The Brave (1991) and The Chief (1993) are companion novels.

BEFORE READING

Ask the group to define "contender." Then have them list at least five qualities of a contender. Have them consider these qualities as they read the novel.

SHARED DISCUSSION

- Robert Lipsyte uses symbolism to communicate the theme of the novel. What does the cave in the park symbolize? What do the stairs to the gym symbolize?
- Alfred says, "What am I, James' shadow or something? I don't need him." Why does Alfred try to hold on to his friendship with James, regardless of James's attitude?
- Debate whether Alfred is jealous of James's relationship with Major.
- What is a "squealer's scar"? What gives Alfred the courage to refuse to unhook the burglar alarm at the Epsteins' store?
- How does Mr. Donatelli describe a contender?
- What does Mr. Donatelli mean when he says, "Anyone can be taught how to fight. A contender, that you have to do yourself"?
- The book has been challenged because James is using drugs. How

are drugs a very real part of Alfred and James's environment? Contrast the way James and Alfred live within this environment.

- Others have challenged the book because it "lacks middle-class African American role models." Alfred is certainly as poor as James, but he does have role models. Debate whether Aunt Pearl is a role model. How is Mr. Donatelli a role model? Why is it unfair to assume that poor kids like Alfred don't have role models?

WRITING PROMPTS AND ACTIVITIES

- Read Langston Hughes's poem "Mother to Son." Think about how Alfred's relationship with Aunt Pearl compares with the relationship of the mother and child in the poem. Choose any two characters in the novel and write a poem about their relationship.
- Write a journal entry that discusses in what ways other than boxing Alfred shows signs of being a contender.
- After James breaks into the grocery store, the Epsteins won't trust Alfred enough to send him to the bank for them. Write a letter that Alfred might write to the Epsteins asking them to reinstate their trust.
- Uncle Wilson says to Alfred, "The trades is opening up." List some trades that offer good opportunities for kids like Alfred. Research places in your community where one can go to prepare for a trade; then share the information in class or in your book group.
- The first heavyweight contender was Tom Molineaux, a Virginia slave. Research his life and career, and write an article about him for a historical issue of the *Ring* magazine.

READ-ALIKES

Crutcher, Chris. *Ironman*. 2004. 288 pp. HarperCollins.

Ages 12-up. Bo is training for a triathlon because that helps him deal with his troubled relationship with his father, but a bad encounter with the football coach gets him suspended and enrolled in anger management sessions.

Holt, K. A. *Knockout*. **2018. 339 pp. Chronicle.**

Ages 12–up. In this novel written in shaped poetry, Levi is medically challenged, but he finds a way to define himself in the boxing ring. The issue is that his mother doesn't know what he's up to until it's too late to keep him from discovering how he might impact the world.

Myers, Walter Dean. *Scorpions*. **2013. 240 pp. Amistad, an imprint of HarperCollins.**

Ages 12–up. Jamal Hicks is the protagonist in this Newbery Honor book set in Harlem, where the Scorpions, a gun-toting gang, pressure kids like Jamal to drop out of school and sign on with them as they bring terror to the neighborhood.

Oaks, J. Adams. *Why I Fight*. **2009. 240 pp. Atheneum/Richard Jackson Books, an imprint of Simon & Schuster.**

Ages 14–up. Eighteen-year-old Wyatt has been crisscrossing the country with Uncle Spade for six years while his uncle tries to turn him into a boxer he doesn't want to be.

Reynolds, Jason. *Ghost*. **2016. 192 pp. Atheneum/Caitlyn Dlouhy Books, an imprint of Simon & Schuster.**

Ages 12–up. Castle "Ghost" Cranshaw has been running since the day his father fired a shot at him, and if he manages to control his emotions and quit fighting, he has the chance to run track at his middle school.

PART IV

OTHER CULTURES AND OTHER LANDS

Other cultures are indeed an important part of the rich heritage of the United States. Immigrants and indigenous people sometimes live by the values and ways of their ancestors while seeking new opportunities in a society that may be foreign to them. These people need to be celebrated. There are critics who question the way other cultures are presented in children's books. These are valid concerns, but it's also important to understand the importance of research and point of view in these novels. Even if there are small inaccuracies in detail, the time and place are key to understanding the big picture. This is certainly the case in *Julie of the Wolves*. Many books about other cultures reflect the cultural background of the writer. These books often reflect the conflict associated with living in a society that doesn't completely accept them and their way of living. Books about other cultures help readers embrace the many cultures that shape their communities.

21 Julie of the Wolves

JEAN CRAIGHEAD GEORGE

She stepped forward on the vast stage at the top of
the world and bowed to her immense audience.

- 1973 NEWBERY MEDAL
- HARPERCOLLINS REISSUE 1997
- 92 PAGES
- AGES 10–14

Left by Kapugen, her widowed father, when she was very young,
Miyax, whose English name is Julie, lives with her Aunt Martha
until she turns thirteen, when she is expected to marry Daniel,
the son of Naka, an Inuk who practices "old-time" traditions. It is June
when Miyax gets the word from the head of Indian Affairs in Mekoryuk
that she is to go to Daniel.

She takes leave of her beloved Aunt Martha and boards a plane for
Barrow, Alaska, where she will meet Daniel for the first time. It turns
out that Daniel is a dull boy who mumbles to himself and tinkers with
his radio. Miyax is told that Daniel will simply be a brother to her, but
one day he comes home in a rage, saying the guys are laughing at him
because he can't mate with his wife, and he tries to rape her. This violent encounter with Daniel finally gives Miyax the courage to escape
her Inuit culture and begin the search for a new life.

In her journey to find a new home, Miyax becomes lost on the
Alaskan tundra and discovers that the only way she can survive
is to become friends with a pack of Arctic wolves. She remembers
that Kapugen had said that wolves are "brotherly" if you learn their

language. She makes a mental note of the leader of the pack, Amaroq, and learns their language and their habits. She becomes one of them until they begin to travel for the winter.

She eventually makes it to civilization, where she learns that Kapugen is no longer living like an Inuk. Instead he has become a hunter, like the one that killed her beloved Amaroq. At this point Miyax is faced with a decision: Does she live the life of an Inuk, or does she live the life her father has chosen for her?

Miyax's story continues in *Julie* (1994) and *Julie's Wolf Pack* (1997).

BEFORE READING

Various cultures and religions have formal coming-of-age ceremonies when a girl and a boy reach a certain age. At one time, in the Inuit culture, a girl was expected to marry at the age of thirteen. Display books about other cultures, and ask readers to find out about the coming-of-age rituals and ceremonies other cultures practice.

SHARED DISCUSSION

- *Julie of the Wolves* is divided into three parts: "Part 1, Amaroq, the wolf"; "Part 2, Miyax, the girl"; and "Part 3, Kapugen, the hunter." Discuss the significance of each part to the overall conflict of the book.
- How does Jean Craighead George use the techniques of flashback and foreshadowing to help readers understand Julie's conflict?
- Miyax's English name is Julie. She didn't mind when the children from Mekoryuk called her Julie. She didn't even mind when her mother called her by her English name. Why does she mind when her father, Kapugen, calls her Julie?
- How does Miyax know that she can learn to communicate with the wolves? Explain how she teaches herself the wolf language. What

makes her choose the black wolf to communicate with first? Why does she think he possesses "wisdom"?

- What does Miyax mean when she says that Jello's actions are "the manner of the lone wolf"?

- Why is Miyax frightened when she learns that her father is still alive? How does she still need him? At the end of the novel, "Julie pointed her boots toward Kapugen." How does this decision help to resolve her conflict?

- *Julie of the Wolves* has been challenged in many schools because of what has been defined as an "attempted rape scene." Discuss why Daniel's attempt to "mate with" Julie might be considered violent in the eyes of some readers. Discuss whether Daniel means to be rough with Julie. How does the scene ultimately change Julie's life?

- There are critics who are now questioning how George portrays the Inuit people, and they don't believe the book should be on library shelves. *Julie of the Wolves* was written in 1972 and is considered a modern classic. Debate whether there may be differences in the Inuit culture since George wrote the novel. Make a list of all the Inuit customs that Miyax practices. Which of these customs are likely not practiced today? How would you answer censors who question the book for cultural reasons?

WRITING PROMPTS AND ACTIVITIES

- "Miyax had felt the bleakness of being left behind once before." Write a journal entry that relates the times that Miyax feels left behind. Write a concluding paragraph that explains why her choice in the end makes her feel left behind once again.

- Write an essay that interprets what Miyax means when she says, "Daylight is spelled A-M-Y."

- Write a letter that Julie might have written to her pen pal, Amy, about her life with the wolves.
- Write a brief journal entry that explains the following metaphor: "She stepped forward on the vast stage at the top of the world and bowed to her immense audience." What is the stage? Who is Miyax's audience?
- Fairy tales and folktales often portray wolves as bad. Write Julie's story as a folktale, portraying the wolf as a hero rather than a villain.

READ-ALIKES

Craig, Ruth. *Malu's Wolf*. 1995. 192 pp. Scholastic.

Ages 9–12. Malu, a young Cro-Magnon girl, raises a young wolf pup after the mother is killed. Tension builds when Gunto, a young hunter, provokes the wolf. When the wolf bites him, Gunto demands that it be killed.

George, Jean Craighead. *Water Sky*. 1989. 224 pp. HarperCollins.

Ages 10-up. Lincoln Noah Stonewright leaves the comforts of his Massachusetts home to spend a few months at a whaling camp in Barrow, Alaska, where he begins exploring his own Inuit heritage.

Hall, Elizabeth. *Child of the Wolves*. 1996. 176 pp. Random House, an imprint of Penguin Random House.

Ages 10-up. A Siberian husky puppy escapes a kennel and is alone in the Alaskan wilderness until Snowdrift, a great white wolf, invites him into the pack.

Hoyt-Goldsmith, Diane. Illus. by Lawrence Migdale. *Arctic Hunter*. 1992. 30 pp. Holiday House.

Ages 8-up. Reggie, a ten-year-old Inupiat boy, describes the camp in Alaska where his family spends each summer hunting and fishing for foods that will last them through the winter months.

Paulsen, Gary. *Dogsong*. 2007. 192 pp. Simon Pulse, an imprint of Simon & Schuster.

Ages 10-up. Russel's father has given up the "old ways" for a new way of life, but Russel wants something more. He takes the sled dogs and hunting equipment that Oogruk, the old man in the village, gives him and sets out on his own to become a man.

Kira-Kira

CYNTHIA KADOHATA

My sister had taught me to look at the world that way, as a place that glitters, as a place where the calls of the crickets and the crows and the wind are everyday occurrences that also happen to be magic.

- 2005 NEWBERY MEDAL
- ATHENEUM, AN IMPRINT OF SIMON & SCHUSTER 2006
- 272 PAGES
- AGES 10–12

Katie Takeshima is about to enter kindergarten in the 1950s when her parents close their Asian foods grocery store in Iowa and move to the small town of Chesterfield, Georgia, to work in a chicken hatchery. Uncle Katsuhisa helps them move into a small apartment complex where other Japanese families live, and they begin a long struggle toward saving money to purchase a house of their own. The working conditions are almost intolerable at the hatchery, and the Japanese Americans run head-on into a boss who mistreats them and union workers who ask them to join the fight for fair pay and a better work environment.

Because Mr. and Mrs. Takeshima work double shifts, Katie and her younger brother, Sammy, are left in the care of their older sister, Lynn. Katie is the only Japanese American student in her class, and she deals with prejudice on a daily basis. Because of this, she relies on Lynn to be her friend. When Lynn becomes a teenager, she makes friends of her own and begins enjoying teenage things like beauty products and clothes. Katie struggles to understand what has happened to the sister who taught her things like kira-kira, the Japanese word for "glitter."

In Katie's mind Lynn is a genius, and she begins to listen as her sister encourages her to be a good student and to look beyond tomorrow. But there is no tomorrow for Lynn. When she is fourteen, and Katie ten, Lynn becomes ill with lymphoma and ultimately dies. At this point, the Takeshima family begins to buckle with grief, but Katie remembers Lynn's special way of looking at life and finds a way to show her parents that there is always hope and something glittering—*kira-kira*—in their future.

BEFORE READING

Kira-kira means "glitter" in Japanese. Ask readers to describe something that is *kira-kira* to them. Examples may include the ocean, stars, the moon, the morning dew on the grass, a dancer under a spotlight, etc.

SHARED DISCUSSION

- Mrs. Takeshima is troubled by how "un-Japanese" her daughters seem, and she vows to one day send them back to Japan. Debate how difficult it was in the early 1950s to belong to one culture and live in another. Why is Mrs. Takeshima so fearful that her daughters will lose their sense of heritage?
- Discuss Katie and Lynn's relationship. Why does Katie feel that her parents like Lynn best? It's Lynn who tells Katie that they are moving to Georgia, and it's Lynn who tells her that their mother is pregnant. Why do Mr. and Mrs. Takeshima leave such important discussions up to Lynn? At what point do Lynn and Katie switch roles?
- Describe the sense of community among the Japanese families in Chesterfield, Georgia. Mr. Kanagawa is considered the leader of the community. How is his leadership revealed in the novel? How does Lynn become the leader of the children in the community?

- How does Mr. Lyndon treat the workers at the hatchery? Some of the workers are trying to unionize so that they can demand better working conditions. Mrs. Takeshima avoids these people because she feels that it's wrong to fight the people who are trying to help you. Why does she feel that Mr. Lyndon is trying to help them? Explain why Mr. and Mrs. Takeshima attend the pro-union meeting at the end of the novel.

- Prejudice is an underlying theme in the novel. The first time that Katie experiences prejudice is at the motel in Tennessee when her family is moving to Georgia. Why does Mr. Takeshima quietly give in to the motel clerk and take the room in the back? Discuss how this is similar to what was happening with African Americans in the Jim Crow South.

- Some adults don't want their children reading about other cultures. How is this a blatant form of prejudice?

- Hitting, stealing, and lying are the three worst crimes to Mr. and Mrs. Takeshima. How does Katie commit each of these crimes in the course of the novel? Discuss the scene where Katie steals pink nail polish for Lynn. How does she justify this crime to herself? Debate whether scenes involving lying and stealing might be one reason some parents have challenged the novel. Debate whether lying and stealing are ever justified. How should those who challenge the book consider Mr. and Mrs. Takeshima and their beliefs regarding the crime?

- Adults who have voiced issues with the novel are concerned about the sadness that the Takeshima family endures. What are the elements of hope in the novel? Explain why it's important to focus on that hope.

WRITING PROMPTS AND ACTIVITIES

- Write a journal entry that discusses the customs practiced by the Takeshima family that demonstrate the family's loyalty to their native culture.

- Think about Uncle Katsuhisa's roles in the family. *Katsu* means "triumph" in Japanese. Write a journal entry that reveals how Uncle Katsuhisa lives up to his name.
- Foreshadowing is a literary device that hints at events that come later in the novel. Lynn wakes up crying one night and says that in her dream she is swimming in the ocean. Write a brief journal entry that discusses what this scene foreshadows.
- Mrs. Takeshima feels that her girls must return to Japan to learn about their femininity. Research the role of women in Japan today. Write a brief article that might appear in a book called *Women in Other Cultures*.
- Lynn always wanted to go to the ocean in California. Write a haiku titled "*Kira-Kira*" that Katie might write and dedicate to Lynn after her family returns from the West Coast.

READ-ALIKES

Jiménez, Francisco. *Breaking Through*. 2002. 208 pp. Houghton Mifflin Harcourt.

Ages 12–up. This sequel to *The Circuit* is a fictionalized memoir of the author's teenage years working migrant labor and enduring extreme prejudice as a Mexican American in California in the 1950s.

Kadohata, Cynthia. *The Thing About Luck*. 2013. 288 pp. Simon & Schuster.

Ages 12–up. When their parents take time off as migrant laborers and return to Japan to care for an ailing relative, Summer and her little brother are left with their grandparents, who came out of retirement to harvest wheat in order to pay the bills.

Kadohata, Cynthia. *Weedflower*. 2006. 272 pp. Atheneum, an imprint of Simon & Schuster.

Ages 12–up. Twelve-year-old Sumiko is the only Japanese girl in her class, and the one thing that eases the pain of the racial slurs from her classmates is the flowers that await her on her California farm. Then World War II breaks out, and Sumiko and her family are forced into an internment camp.

Lowry, Lois. *A Summer to Die*. 2016 (reissue). 192 pp. Houghton Mifflin Harcourt.

Ages 12-up. Thirteen-year-old Meg and her older sister, Molly, are extremely different. Molly is pretty and popular, and when she is diagnosed with leukemia, insecure Meg must find a way to deal with her sister's illness and impending death.

Sánchez, Erika L. *I Am Not Your Perfect Mexican Daughter*. 2017. 352 pp. Knopf, an imprint of Penguin Random House.

Ages 12-up. Unlike her older sister, Olga, Julia doesn't care so much for her family's Mexican traditions. While grieving Olga's death from a car accident, Julia becomes determined to live her real American dream and leave her parents' Chicago home to attend college.

TEACHER'S GUIDE

A Complete Teacher's Guide is available on

the publisher's website.

American Born Chinese

GENE LUEN YANG

ILLUSTRATED BY GENE LUEN YANG AND LARK PIEN

You misunderstood my intentions, Jin. I did not come to punish you. I came to serve as your conscience—as a signpost to your soul.

- 2007 MICHAEL L. PRINTZ AWARD
- ROARING BROOK, AN IMPRINT OF MACMILLAN 2007
- 240 PAGES
- AGES 12-UP

This graphic novel about self-identity and learning to cope cultural stereotypes is told in three stories: "The Monkey King," "Jin Wang," and "Danny and Chin-Kee." There is a connection between the stories, and by the end of the novel readers realize the overall message that takes them from ancient China to the present.

"The Monkey King" is an ancient Chinese fable about a monkey who believes he should be king of Flower-Fruit Mountain. His is a kung fu master and uses his skill to hop on a cloud and make his demands known. The guards aren't impressed with the monkey, and they banish him from the kingdom. Tze-Yo-Tzuh, the supreme god, punishes the monkey by locking him away for five hundred years in a mountain cave. He is eventually saved by a Buddhist monk who sets out to teach monkey the virtue of humility.

"Jin Wang," set in present-day San Francisco's Chinatown, is about the story's titular Chinese American character and his struggles to belong in his new neighborhood. Jin Wang looks different, his accent makes him an outsider, and his mother sends him to school with "odd" foods in his lunchbox. On the very first day of school, he is bullied on the playground. He reacts by acting mean toward Wei-Chen, a new boy from Taiwan, in hopes that this behavior will elevate him in the eyes of his white classmates.

"Danny and Chin-Kee," the final story, focuses on a white American teenager and his Chinese cousin, Chin-Kee. When Chin-Kee arrives at Danny's house with his clothes packed in Chinese food takeout boxes, Danny is embarrassed to claim him as a relative. To Danny, Chin-Kee possesses all of the typical Chinese stereotypes: yellow skin, hair in a long braid, poor English, and traditional clothing. Danny is worried about being associated with Chin-Kee, and in an effort to avoid mockery from classmates, Danny moves to another school where he might have a chance to be a popular kid and a star basketball player.

In the concluding pages of the novel, it's revealed that Danny is really Jin, who transformed himself as a way of dealing with his cultural identity. Wei-Chen is the human son of the Monkey King who was sent to America to aid Danny on his personal journey. Finally, Jin accepts his Chinese American identity and eventually apologizes to Wei-Chen, who by now is his friend.

BEFORE READING

Ask readers to discuss why it is difficult for adolescents from a different culture to fit in at a typical American high school. Brainstorm what schools and students can do to make these teens feel welcome. Allow readers to work with partners and role-play a scene where they invite a "new" student from a different culture to participate in a school event.

SHARED DISCUSSION

- Explain the structure of the novel. What is the role of the Monkey King? Discuss why Yang tells Chin-Kee's story as a television show. Discuss how the three stories converge for a larger meaning in the end.

- Jin is struggling with his Chinese American identity. Why is it significant to Jin's story that he cannot speak Chinese? In what ways is Jin a typical American adolescent? What is the purpose of the scene where Jin kisses Wei-Chen's girlfriend?

- Explain why Danny is embarrassed by his cousin, Wei-Chen. What is Wei-Chen's role in helping Jin confront issues related to self-identity?

- Contrast Jin's new life to his life in San Francisco's Chinatown. Why is assimilating to another environment difficult for him? Debate whether he feels stuck in two worlds.

- How is Jin the target of bullies? Explain how he plays out this experience by becoming another character. Discuss how he becomes the bully when he assumes the role of Danny.

- The novel has been challenged because of "its blatant stereotyping of the Chinese culture." Cite the use of stereotypes in the story. How are these stereotypes used to convey Jin's personal conflict?

- Scenes with bullying those who are different is another issue that some adults raise with the novel. Discuss the incidents of bullying in the book. How does Yang use bullying to communicate issues related to cultural awareness and self-identity? What message is Yang sending readers about tolerance?

- Craft an appropriate statement to a school board that may be dealing with a challenge to this novel. Explain how teens might view Yang's novel as a cautionary story.

WRITING PROMPTS AND ACTIVITIES

- Define "irony." Then write an essay about the author's use of irony in the story. Cite specific scenes, and use direct quotes to support your thoughts.

- Write a journal entry that discusses the way humor in illustration and text conveys the theme of cultural identity. Cite specific scenes and use direct quotes from the novel to support your thoughts.
- Wei-Chen is the alter ego of Jin. Write a letter that Wei-Chen might write to Jin about taking pride in his Chinese culture.
- Think about the reference to the Christmas story in Chapter 8 of the book. Write a journal entry that discusses the contribution of this biblical story to the overall meaning of the novel.
- *American Born Chinese* won the 2007 Michael L. Printz Award and was a finalist for the 2006 National Book Award in the category of Young People's Literature. Think about the literary qualities of the novel, and write remarks about the book for the awards ceremonies. Include comments about the illustrations.

READ-ALIKES

de la Peña, Matt. *Mexican WhiteBoy*. 2010. 272 pp. Ember, an imprint of Penguin Random House.

Ages 12-up. Danny Lopez is an outsider in his Mexican father's family and in the white private school where he is a star baseball player. He spends the summer with the Mexican half of his family and befriends Uno, a biracial boy who also struggles with cultural identity.

Edwardson, Debby Dahl. *My Name Is Not Easy*. 2013. 256 pp. Skyscape, an imprint of Amazon Publishing.

Ages 12-up. Set in Alaska in the 1960s, Luke Aaluk, an Inupiaq boy, is sent to a Catholic boarding school where his culture is unappreciated. Racism and bullying engulf his life, and he struggles to understand where he belongs.

Hidier, Tanuja Desai. *Born Confused*. 2014. 512 pp. Push, an imprint of Scholastic.

Ages 14-up. Dimple Lala spends her seventeenth summer in a

personal struggle. She has grown up in Springfield, New York, and feels American, but her immigrant parents still follow India's traditions.

Khorram, Adib. *Darius the Great Is Not Okay*. **2018. 320 pp. Dial, an imprint of Penguin Random House.**

Ages 12-up. Darius Kellner is a sophomore in an Oregon high school where he is bullied because of his part-Iranian heritage and his struggle with clinical depression. When his family travels to Iran to be with a dying relative, Darius forms an unexpected friendship and finally learns what it means to belong.

Yoon, David. *Frankly in Love*. **2019. 406 pp. Putnam, an imprint of Penguin Random House.**

Ages 14-up. Frank Li was born in the United States, but his Korean parents still call him Sung-Min Li, his Korean name. They expect him to observe Korean traditions and to one day marry a Korean girl. The problem is that Frank is in love with the American girl of his dreams, Brit Means.

PART V

THE PAST AND THE FUTURE

The past has been riddled with controversy. It may be the loyalties and disloyalties in wars that formed this nation, eras like the Great Depression that brought poverty to many American citizens, the brutality of the Holocaust, or the practice of witchcraft during the Middle Ages and even in American during the 1690s. Nevertheless, novels set during these periods bring history alive to young readers, something that textbooks alone cannot do. Reading about the future is equally important. Science fiction about utopian and dystopian communities and ethical issues such as cloning challenges readers to think about what is possible in the realm of science. These novels point readers into worlds they may not otherwise explore.

24 Bud, Not Buddy

CHRISTOPHER PAUL CURTIS

There comes a time when you're losing a fight that it just doesn't make sense to keep on fighting. It's not that you're being a quitter; it's just that you've got the sense to know when enough is enough.

- 2000 NEWBERY MEDAL
- DELACORTE, AN IMPRINT OF PENGUIN RANDOM HOUSE 1999
- 288 PAGES
- AGES 9–12

Set during the Great Depression in Flint, Michigan, ten-year-old Bud Caldwell has lived in an orphanage and several foster homes since the death of his mother when he was six. His only possession is a cardboard suitcase filled with memories of his mother: a blanket, a photograph of his mother as a child, a bag of rocks, and a flyer about the Dusky Devastators, a jazz band led by bass player Herman E. Calloway. He also has in his head a list of life lessons that he calls "Bud Caldwell's Rules and Things for Having a Funner Life and Making a Better Liar Out of Yourself."

The orphanage and previous foster homes haven't worked out so well for Bud. Now he has been placed with the Amoses, who have a twelve-year-old son who immediately launches an attack on Bud. When the two boys get into a fight, Mrs. Amos blames Bud, and Mr. Amos locks him in the garden shed for the night. He breaks out of the shed, sneaks into the house for his suitcase, and manages to get revenge on Todd Amos before he runs away. He comes upon Bugs, an old friend from the home, who plans to ride the rails west. He convinces Bud to come along, but Bugs makes it onto the moving train and Bud doesn't.

Bud sleeps under a tree outside the library, eats breakfast at a mission, and makes a plan to walk to Grand Rapids, Michigan, in search of Herman E. Calloway, the man who he believes is his father. With the kind help of a few people, including a man named Lefty Lewis, Bud reaches his destination and locates Calloway. The famous musician denies Bud's claim that he is his father. Bud takes clues from the contents of his suitcase and finds that Calloway is instead his grandfather. Finally, Bud has the home he needs, and he sleeps in the bedroom that was once his mother's.

BEFORE READING

Explain to readers that *Bud, Not Buddy* is set during the Great Depression. Ask them what they know about this era. Tell them that Bud, the main character in the novel, is homeless and goes to a mission for a hot meal. Have readers find out what organizations in their city or town provide food and shelter for the homeless today.

SHARED DISCUSSION

- Discuss Bud's relationship with his mother. What are some of his special memories of her? Why do you think Bud's mother changed her name and left home? Discuss why she never told Bud about his grandfather. If she was so unhappy, why did she keep the flyers about her dad's band?
- Bud has been without a family since age six. What survival skills does he learn at the Home?
- Make a list of "Bud Caldwell's Rules and Things for Having a Funner Life and Making a Better Liar Out of Yourself." How does Bud use these rules to survive difficult situations?
- Bud's mother once told him, "When one door closes, don't worry, because another door opens." How does this statement give Bud

the hope he needs to search for his father? At what point does the door open?

- Cite evidence that Herman Calloway had hope that his daughter might return.
- The novel has been challenged for "racism." Mrs. Amos uses the word "boy" when she addresses Bud. How is this racist language? Explain how this defines her character.
- The book has also been challenged for "violence." Cite specific "violent" scenes. How do these scenes influence Bud's journey to search for his family?
- How would you explain Bud's character and his quest for family to censors?

WRITING PROMPTS AND ACTIVITIES

- Bud has special memories of his mother reading to him. He remembers the little lessons that he learned from the fables that she read. Select one of "Bud Caldwell's Rules and Things for Having a Funner Life and Making a Better Liar Out of Yourself" and write a fable, using the rule as the lesson learned.
- Write a journal entry that explains the following metaphor: "The idea that had started as a teeny-weeny seed in a suitcase was now a mighty maple." What is the seed? The mighty maple?
- Write a brief essay that explains how the flyers in Bud's suitcase give him hope.
- Mrs. Amos says, "I do not have time to put up with the foolishness of those members of our race who do not want to be uplifted." Write a journal entry that discusses how this statement indicates that Mrs. Amos feels superior to Bud and other members of her race. Include a concluding paragraph that expresses why she thinks Bud doesn't want to be uplifted.

- Entertainment played a major role during the Great Depression. One of Bud's flyers describes Calloway's Band as "Masters of the New Jazz." In small groups, use books in the library and sites on the internet to find out who the major jazz artists were during the Great Depression. Present information on one band or individual artist to the class. If possible, share music they were best known for.

READ-ALIKES

Curtis, Christopher Paul. *The Mighty Miss Malone*. 320 pp. 2012. Wendy Lamb Books, an imprint of Penguin Random House.

Ages 9–12. Deza Malone, first introduced in *Bud, Not Buddy*, and her mother wind up in a Hooverville shack when they go in search of her father, who left Gary, Indiana, for Flint, Michigan, in hopes of finding work.

De Young, C. Coco. *A Letter to Mrs. Roosevelt*. 2000. 112 pp. Yearling, an imprint of Penguin Random House.

Ages 8–10. Set in Johnstown, Pennsylvania, during the Great Depression, eleven-year-old Margo Bandini's family is about to lose their home, and she is determined to find a way to help. She writes a letter to Mrs. Roosevelt, and her family receives an emergency loan.

Fox, Paula. *Monkey Island*. 1991. 160 pp. Orchard Books, an imprint of Scholastic.

Ages 9–12. Eleven-year-old Clay Garrity waits in a shabby hotel for his mother before he gives up and begins sleeping in a cardboard box in the park.

Holman, Felice. *Slake's Limbo*. 1986. 125 pp. Aladdin, an imprint of Simon & Schuster.

Ages 9–12. Thirteen-year-old Aremis Slake is motherless and manages to make a home in a wall of the New York subway. He resells newspapers and gets a job sweeping a luncheonette for food.

Philbrick, Rodman. *Zane and the Hurricane: A Story of Katina.* **2014. 192 pp. The Blue Sky Press, an imprint of Scholastic.**

Ages 9–12. Zane Dupree is twelve years old when he goes to New Orleans to visit his great-grandmother, his only link to his dead father. When Hurricane Katrina hits the city, the two are left to survive the rising waters.

My Brother Sam Is Dead

JAMES LINCOLN COLLIER AND
CHRISTOPHER COLLIER

I'd stand at the door and watch them go; and I wondered, if I went.for a soldier, which army would I join? The British had the best uniforms and the shiny new guns, but there was something exciting about the Patriots—being underdogs and fighting off the mighty British army.

- 1975 NEWBERY HONOR
- SIMON & SCHUSTER 1974
- 224 PAGES
- AGES 10–14

Tim Meeker is sixty-four years old in 1826 when he records his memories of the bloody American Revolution and how it split his family apart. All of his life he had looked up to his older brother, Sam. At sixteen years old, Sam, known for his intelligence, is a student at Yale College. Life Meeker, the boys' father, is proud of Sam until the day he shows up at the family farm in Redding, Connecticut, and announces that he has quit school to join the Continental army. Tim, on the other hand, is smitten with Sam's uniform and thinks that Sam looks brave. Sam and his father exchange bitter words about the war, and Sam tells Tim the real reason that he came home. He has come to get the "Brown Bess," a gun that belongs to his father, to use as his weapon in the war.

Life Meeker disowns Sam, while Tim and his mother worry and don't mention Sam's name in Life's presence. As the war progresses, Tim begins to realize that his father is not so much a Tory as he is against war. He sees no use for violence, and he doesn't think that any political issue is worth losing innocent lives for.

When Tim accompanies his father to New York to get supplies

for his tavern, they encounter cowboys, and Life Meeker is taken prisoner for selling beef to the British. He dies of cholera on board a prison ship. The British march into Redding and kill some of Tim's close friends, and Sam is publicly shot after he is captured for "stealing cattle."

Tim becomes sickened with the entire idea of the war and the violence that has broken apart his family. He remembers a stern father and a stubborn and brave older brother. He remembers his mother's broken heart at the loss of her husband and her oldest son. And he wonders "if there might have been another way, beside war, to achieve the same end."

BEFORE READING

Read aloud "Paul Revere's Ride" by Henry Wadsworth Longfellow. Discuss Revere's mission. On April 19, 1775, the first shot is taken, and the American Revolution begins. Engage readers in a discussion about why that shot is referred to as the "shot heard around the world."

SHARED DISCUSSION

- At the beginning of the novel, Sam is trying to explain to his father that the first shot, signaling the beginning of the American Revolution, has been taken. His father asks, "Who do you think fired first?" Sam cannot answer the question and doesn't understand why it matters. Why does it matter to Life Meeker to know who fired first? Why doesn't it matter to Sam?
- Sam's father asks, "Is it worth war to save a few pence in taxes?" Sam replies, "It's not the money, it's the principle." To what principle is Sam referring? How are most wars about principle?
- At what point in the novel does the war become real to Tim?
- Tim is nervous about seeing Sam after their father is captured. He

says, "For the first time in my life I knew that Sam was wrong about something. I knew that I understood something better than he did." Discuss what Tim feels that he understands.

- What does Life Meeker mean when he says, "In war the dead pay the debts for the living"? Tim feels that before his father died, he had forgiven Sam. Why does Tim blame Sam for Life Meeker's death?

- *My Brother Sam Is Dead* has been challenged in schools because of "the graphic violence." How can there be an accurate depiction of war without violence?

- Sam and his father have a very angry exchange of words. Profanity is used, which has caused some parents to challenge the use of the novel in schools. How does the profanity communicate the outrage between father and son?

- Some adults feel the book is "unpatriotic" because Life Meeker disapproves of the war that brought the United States to independence. Discuss how there are always two sides to war. Explain Tim's view of war at the end of the novel. Debate how difficult it would be to stand by and watch war tear one's family apart.

WRITING PROMPTS AND ACTIVITIES

- Define "treason." Sam states that Massachusetts and Connecticut are ready to fight. Sam's father says that such a discussion is treason. How are Sam and Life's definitions of treason different? Write a journal entry that compares their views. Use direct quotes and cite passages from the novel to support your thoughts.

- Patrick Henry delivered his famous "Give me liberty, or give me death" speech on March 23, 1775. Write a story about this speech that might have appeared in a patriot newspaper.

- At the end of the novel, Sam is executed. Write a eulogy that Tim might have written for Sam.

- Tim is an old man when he relates the story of how the war changed his family. Think of all the ways the war changed Tim. Then write a journal entry that traces Tim's passage from boyhood to manhood.

- *My Brother Sam Is Dead* has been challenged in schools because some parents feel that the book "contains an inaccurate depiction of the Revolutionary War." Write down all the facts about the Revolutionary War that are revealed in the book. Then use books in the library or sites on the internet to document these facts. Discuss whether the parents' complaints are valid.

READ-ALIKES

Avi. *The Fighting Ground*. 2009. 160 pp. HarperCollins.

Ages 10–12. Thirteen-year-old Jonathan thinks war is glamorous until April 3, 1778, when he is taken prisoner and must wrestle with his own feelings about killing and the horrors of war.

Collier, James Lincoln, and Christopher Collier. *War Comes to Willy Freeman*. 1987. 192 pp. Random House, an imprint of Penguin Random House.

Ages 10–14. Willy Freeman, a young African American girl, watches as the redcoats kill her father, and she returns home to discover that the British have taken her mother prisoner.

Elliott, L. M. *Give Me Liberty*. 2008. 384 pp. HarperCollins.

Ages 10–14. Set in 1774, thirteen-year-old Nathaniel, an indentured servant, joins the Patriot army as a fifer and ends up at the Battle of Great Bridge, where he comes face-to-face with some people from his past and the British army.

Fritz, Jean. Illus. by Lynd Ward. *Early Thunder*. 1987. 256 pp. Penguin, an imprint of Penguin Random House.

Ages 10–14. As the people in the colonies are choosing sides, a boy in Salem struggles with his decision and shifts his loyalty from King George to the patriots.

Orgill, Roxane. *Siege: How General Washington Kicked the British Out of Boston and Launched a Revolution.* **2018. 240 pp. Candlewick.** Ages 10–14. Set in 1775 when the British occupied Boston, this novel in verse relates the stories of American Revolutionary personalities like George Washington, Henry Knox, and Abigail Adams.

26 The Midwife's Apprentice

KAREN CUSHMAN

I know how to try and risk and fail and try again and
not give up.

- 1996 NEWBERY MEDAL
- HOUGHTON MIFFLIN HARCOURT 2012
- 144 PAGES
- AGES 10–14

Set in medieval England, a homeless girl with no name except Brat
sleeps in a dung heap and scavenges around for food scraps to
ease her hunger. She doesn't really know her age, but because her
body is beginning to show signs of becoming a woman, she is maybe
twelve or thirteen.

One day she meets Jane Sharp, the village midwife, who calls her
Beetle because she resembles a dung beetle that burrows in the heap.
The girl convinces the reluctant midwife that she will work for food
and shelter, and she soon becomes the midwife's apprentice. Jane is
sharp-tongued and harsh and treats Beetle like a dimwit. When Beetle
saves Will Russet, a village boy who bullied her, from drowning, he
becomes nicer and names her Alyce. But Alyce runs away after she is
unsuccessful while assisting a birth, and she finds a job at an inn in a
neighboring village. By her side is a stray cat that she adopted when
she was in the heap.

Jane Sharp happens by the inn and tells the innkeeper that Beetle
wasn't what she needed because she gave up when things got tough.
Then, on the first of June, a group of prosperous-looking people stop

at the inn seeking help for the wife of one of the men. They believe she has a stomach worm, but Alyce quickly realizes the woman is about to have a baby. Remembering the skills she had learned from Jane Sharp, Alyce goes into action and delivers a healthy baby. She is praised and offered employment as a nursemaid, but instead she returns to Jane Sharp and declares that she will be a good apprentice now.

BEFORE READING

Tell readers that the term *midwife* means "with woman." Explain what "with woman" means. Historically, almost all pregnant women were attended by midwives. Then discuss the difference between a midwife and doula. How do many midwives also take on the role of doula?

SHARED DISCUSSION

- Describe Jane Sharp. Why is she reluctant to take in Brat? Discuss whether her sharp tongue and harshness suggest that she is an unhappy woman. What might have contributed to her unhappiness? How is she cruel to the women giving birth?

- "This business of having a name was harder than it seemed. A name was of little use if no one would call you by it." Why is having a name, rather than a nickname, important to Brat? Explain the significance of receiving a name from Will Russet. Debate whether Jane Sharp will call her Alyce rather than Beetle when she resumes her apprenticeship.

- How are Jane Sharp and the innkeeper dishonest? How is their dishonesty about greed? What is Alyce's reaction to their bad practices?

- Explain the symbolism of the open door at the end of the novel.

- What is the role of religion in the medieval village?

- The novel has been censored for "sexual content" because of the phrase "roll in the hay." Define "idiom." How is "roll in the hay" an idiom? What is the literal and figurative meaning of the phrase?

- To what are censors referring when they voice opposition to the novel because of "mysticism or paganism"? Discuss the superstitious beliefs of the villagers. How are these superstitions connected to their religious practices? Discuss how these superstitions contribute to a reader's understanding of the historical period.

- Why do the villagers feel they are targets of the Devil? How does Alyce know about the sins of the villagers? What are the sins of Jane Sharp and the Baker? Discuss Alyce's "goodness." Explain how the censors should focus on Alyce, rather than on the "evil" characters.

WRITING PROMPTS AND ACTIVITIES

- What is Beetle's definition of a witch? Write a brief journal entry that explains why she thinks that Jane Sharp is a witch. Support your thoughts by making specific references to the text.

- The cook at the inn tells Edward that a story should have a "hero and brave deeds." Select a character other than Alyce and write a two-page short story about the heroism and brave deeds of the character.

- Write a short journal entry that traces the personal journey of Alyce from the beginning of the novel to the end. How does she grow as a person?

- One of the central themes of the novel is the search for identity. Write a short journal entry that discusses the relationship between the "need to belong" and the "search for identity." Make specific references to Alyce's journey to support your thoughts.

- Use books in the library and sites on the internet to research life in medieval times. Then use this information and information garnered from the novel to create a PowerPoint presentation titled "Daily Life in Medieval Times."

READ-ALIKES

Avi. *Crispin: The Cross of Lead*. **2004. 320 pp. Hyperion.**

Ages 10–14. This 2003 Newbery Medal winner is set in fourteenth-century England, and it tells the story of a peasant boy who has no name until at his mother's death a priest reveals that his name is Crispin. The boy finds himself in grave danger when his mortal enemy declares him "wolf's-head," a term that means anyone's prey.

Cushman, Karen. *Catherine, Called Birdy*. **2019. 192 pp. Houghton Mifflin Harcourt.**

Ages 10–14. At the suggestion of her brother, fourteen-year-old Catherine, the daughter of an impoverished knight, keeps a diary so that she may learn to be less childish. Set in the year 1290, this 1995 Newbery Honor book depicts medieval life.

Cushman, Karen. *Matilda Bone*. **2014. 176 pp. Houghton Mifflin Harcourt.**

Ages 10–14. Set in medieval London, Matilda, an orphaned girl raised by a priest, takes up life in Blood and Bone Alley, when she is apprenticed to Red Peg the Bonesetter.

Park, Linda Sue. *A Single Shard*. **2001. 160 pp. Houghton Mifflin Harcourt.**

Ages 10–14. Set in the twelfth century in Korea, orphaned Tree-ear lives under a bridge until he becomes an assistant to Min, a master potter. This 2002 Newbery Medal book takes readers back in time and introduces them to the famous celadon pottery.

Schlitz, Laura Amy. Illus. by Robert Byrd. *Good Masters! Sweet Ladies! Voices from a Medieval Village*. **2007. 96 pp. Candlewick.**

Ages 10-up. Inspired by the Munich-Nuremberg manuscript, a poem from thirteenth-century Germany, this 2008 Newbery Medal winner is set in 1255 and includes twenty-two portraits of villagers.

27

Chains

LAURIE HALSE ANDERSON

It was like looking at a knot, knowing it was a knot, but not knowing how to untie it. I had no map for this life.

- ATHENEUM, AN IMPRINT OF SIMON & SCHUSTER 2008
- 320 PAGES
- AGES 12-UP

The first book in the Seeds of America trilogy is set in 1776 at the beginning of the American Revolution. Thirteen-year-old Isabel and her younger sister, Ruth, are robbed of the freedom granted them in Miss Mary Finch's will. The girls are forced to leave Newport, Rhode Island, when Miss Mary's nephew, Robert Finch, sells them in an auction to the Locktons, a cruel and ruthless Loyalist family from New York. As the war between the Tories and the Patriots escalates in a city divided in its loyalties, Isabel's personal battles grow.

Madam Lockton, the wife of the new owner, is spooked by Ruth's fits and sends her to another estate they own in Charleston, South Carolina. Isabel is abused and branded for disobedience. Curzon, a slave boy whom Isabel has befriended, convinces her that the only way to freedom is to become a spy for the rebels. As Madam Lockton's harsh treatment gets worse, Isabel begins more spying. She uncovers Mr. Lockton's plan to assassinate General George Washington. He is arrested for treason but is saved by his influential aunt, Lady Seymour.

While this is happening, Curzon is captured and thrown in prison. Feeling lonely and desperate, Isabel is faced with a difficult question:

Should she work for or against the British? When she searches deep within her soul for the answer, she makes a life-changing discovery: She is loyal only to herself.

Isabel visits Curzon in prison and slips food to him to give him strength. She eventually bails him out, and the two cross the river in a battered rowboat to New Jersey and begin their long journey in search of Ruth.

Forge (2010) and *Ashes* (2016) complete the trilogy.

BEFORE READING

Chains is the first book of a trilogy called Seeds of America. How is this series name appropriate for books about the American Revolution? Think about the title of the first book in the series and predict a possible conflict.

SHARED DISCUSSION

- Describe the life of slaves in the American colonies in the 1700s. Discuss the difference between a servant and a slave. How did Miss Mary Finch's view of slavery differ from that of most slave owners?
- Why does Mr. Robert accuse Isabel of lying when she tells him that she read Miss Mary's will? Explain why Pastor Weeks thinks that teaching a slave to read only "leads to trouble."
- Mr. Robert collects Isabel and Ruth on the day of Miss Mary's funeral. Why aren't the girls allowed to take personal items with them? Explain the symbolism of the seeds that Isabel hides in the hem of her dress. She plants the seeds, and one day finds that the plants have died. What do the dead plants represent?
- Role models may be found in real life and in stories. How are Isabel's momma and Queen Esther in the Bible her role models for bravery? Discuss the connection between bravery, courage, and

fear. What is Isabel's first act of bravery? Discuss her most fearful moments. How are her bravery and courage fueled by her fears?

- The Mayor of New York, a Loyalist, says, "The beast has grown too large. If it breaks free of its chains, we are all in danger. We need to cut off its head." Who is the beast? Who is the head? Why is Lockton so adamantly opposed to the mayor's proposal?

- Isabel says, "Madam looked down without seeing me. She did not look into my eyes, did not see the lion inside. She did not see the me of me, the Isabel." What is the lion inside of Isabel? What does Lady Seymour see in Isabel that Madam Lockton doesn't see?

- *Chains* has been challenged in classrooms because it's thought to be "politically offensive." Cite specific scenes for which censors might be troubled. How would you defend these scenes in the novel?

- Others who have challenged the novel call it "racially offensive." Slavery is a very dark side of our nation's history and is therefore offensive. Why is it important to be offended by it? Explain why it's important to read history as it happened.

WRITING PROMPTS AND ACTIVITIES

- Write a journal entry that discusses how Isabel becomes bolder and braver as the novel develops. Support your thoughts by citing specific scenes in the novel.

- Colonel Regan gives Isabel the code word *ad astra* to use when entering the rebel camp. The word means "to the stars" in Latin. Write a journal entry that explains why this is an appropriate code word for the rebels. Include a concluding paragraph that discusses how the word foreshadows Isabel and Curzon's ultimate escape to freedom at the end of the novel.

- Isabel has lived her entire life in bondage but dreams of freedom. Write an essay that reveals Isabel's idea of freedom.

- At the beginning of the novel, Isabel needs Curzon. Write a short journal entry that illustrates how Curzon needs Isabel at the end of the novel. Make specific references to the novel to support your thoughts.
- The old man whom Isabel calls Grandfather says, "Everything that stands between you and freedom is the River Jordan." Write a journal entry that explains the figurative River Jordan in the novel. Include a discussion of all the tributaries that feed into Isabel's River Jordan.

READ-ALIKES

Blackwood, Gary L. *Year of the Hangman*. 2004. 272 pp. Penguin, an imprint of Penguin Random House.

Ages 12-up. The American Revolution has been raging for a year when fifteen-year-old Creighton Brown, a Brit, goes to work for Benjamin Franklin in his printshop and is forced to make a decision about his true loyalties.

Buckley, Gail Lumet. *American Patriots: The Story of Blacks in the Military from the Revolution to Desert Storm*. 2002. 608 pp. Random House, an imprint of Penguin Random House.

Ages 12-up. Adapted for young readers from an adult book by the same title, the struggles and triumphs of Black soldiers who fought for the nation's freedom are illuminated through interviews and other source documents.

Paulsen, Gary. *Woods Runner*. 2011. 176 pp. Wendy Lamb Books, an imprint of Penguin Random House.

Ages 12-up. Set around the time of the Concord and Lexington uprising, thirteen-year-old Samuel returns from hunting in the wilderness near his Pennsylvania home and finds his home burned to the ground and his parents missing. He begins a long search for his parents that takes him to British-held New York.

Rinaldi, Ann. *The Fifth of March: A Story of the Boston Massacre.* **2004. 352 pp. Houghton Mifflin Harcourt.**

Ages 12-up. Rachel Marsh, an indentured servant to John and Abigail Adams, ponders her family's allegiances in the years before the American Revolution and now must struggle to determine her own political thoughts.

Rinaldi, Ann. *Finishing Becca: A Story about Peggy Shippen and Benedict Arnold.* **2004. 384 pp. Houghton Mifflin Harcourt.**

Ages 12-up. Becca Synge is fourteen years old when she goes to work as a maid to Peggy Shippen, who becomes the wife of Benedict Arnold. As the American Revolution is raging all around her, Becca must confront her own loyalties.

TEACHER'S AND BOOK DISCUSSION GUIDE

A complete Teacher's and Book Discussion Guide is available on the publisher's website.

28

The Book Thief

MARKUS ZUSAK

Together, they would watch everything that was so carefully planned collapse, and they would all smile at the beauty of destruction.

- 2007 MICHAEL L. PRINTZ HONOR BOOK
- RANDOM HOUSE, AN IMPRINT OF PENGUIN RANDOM HOUSE 2013
- 592 PAGES
- AGES 14–UP

Told from the point of view of Death and set during the 1930s, Liesel Meminger is only nine years old when she is taken to live with a foster family, Hans and Rosa Hubermann, on Himmel Street in Molching, Germany. She arrives with few possessions, but among them is *The Grave Digger's Handbook,* a book that she stole from the cemetery on the day that her brother was buried. It had fallen from the pocket of a gravedigger.

During the years that Liesel lives with the Hubermanns, Hitler becomes more powerful, life on Himmel Street becomes more fearful, and Liesel becomes a full-fledged book thief. She rescues books from Nazi book burnings and steals from the library of the mayor. Liesel is illiterate when she steals her first book, but Hans Hubermann, whom she calls Papa, uses her prized books to teach her to read.

In time, Liesel believes that Hitler is responsible for her parents' disappearance and her brother's death. She becomes anti-Hitler but is warned by Hans to hide her opinions of the ruthless murderer.

Max Vandenburg, a Jewish fistfighter whose father served in World War I with Hans, takes refuge from the Nazi regime in the basement of the Hubermanns' home, where he develops a close relationship with Liesel. When he is forced to leave, Rosa gives Liesel a book, *The Word Shaker*, that Max wrote for her about their friendship. Now that Liesel is literate, she begins creating her own stories. She is editing her book when the Hubermanns' home is bombed, and she is the only survivor. Since she no longer has a home, Liesel goes to live with the mayor and his wife. She drops the book she has been writing, *The Book Thief*, but it's retrieved by Death.

Liesel lives a long life and leaves behind children and grandchildren. And when she dies, Death returns *The Book Thief* to her as he's taking her soul away.

BEFORE READING

Engage readers in a discussion about the Holocaust. Why did the Nazis have public book burnings? The books they burned were ones that promoted ideologies opposed to Nazism. How was this an attempt to "cleanse" society? Debate the thought that burning books doesn't destroy the ideas expressed in its pages.

SHARED DISCUSSION

- Discuss the symbolism of Death as the omniscient narrator of the novel. What are Death's feelings for each victim? Describe Death's attempt to resist Liesel.
- *The Grave Digger's Handbook* is the first book Liesel steals. Why does she take the book? What is significant about the titles of the books she steals?
- Abandonment is a central theme in the novel. How does Liesel equate love with abandonment? At what point does she understand why her mother abandoned her? Who else abandons Liesel in the novel?

- Death says that Liesel was a girl "with a mountain to climb." What is her mountain? Who are her climbing partners? What is her greatest obstacle? At what point does she reach the summit of her mountain? Describe her descent. What does she discover at the foot of her mountain?

- Guilt is another recurring theme in the novel. Hans Hubermann's life was spared in France during World War I, and Erik Vandenburg's life was taken. Explain why Hans feels guilty about Erik's death. Guilt is a powerful emotion that may cause a person to become unhappy and despondent. Discuss how Hans channels his guilt into helping others.

- *The Book Thief* has concerned parents of students in middle school because of "violence." How can there be a book about the Holocaust and war without violence?

- Explain why it is important to read and study about the Holocaust. Why is no information worse than more information?

- The Nazi burned books in an effort to eradicate independent thought. They wanted to keep people ignorant of things that may be considered "un-German." Discuss the irony of an illiterate girl stealing books that are about to be burned. Censors still sometimes have public book burnings. Discuss how any attempt to close off thought is bad for society.

WRITING PROMPTS AND ACTIVITIES

- Write an essay that discusses why the humans in the novel haunt Death. Cite specific passages from the novel to support your thoughts.

- Define irony. What is ironic about Liesel's obsession with stealing books? Write a journal entry that examines other uses of irony in the novel.

- Consider what was happening in Germany in the 1930s. Write a journal entry that debates whether Liesel was abandoned by circumstance or by the heart.
- Write an analytical journal entry that reveals how Zusak uses the literary device of foreshadowing to pull the reader into the story.
- Liesel Meminger lives to be an old woman. Death says that he would like to tell the book thief about beauty and brutality, but those are things that she had lived. Write a journal entry that discusses how her life represents beauty in the wake of brutality. Make specific references to the novel to support your thoughts.

READ-ALIKES

Hesse, Monica. *Girl in the Blue Coat*. 2016. 320 pp. Little, Brown.

Ages 14-up. Eighteen-year-old Hanneke, the protagonist of this mystery set against the backdrop of the Holocaust, smuggles goods to neighbors but one day is asked to find a missing girl in a blue coat.

Iturbe, Antonio. Translated by Lilit Thwaites. *The Librarian of Auschwitz*. 2017. 432 pp. Holt, an imprint of Macmillan.

Ages 14-up. Fourteen-year-old Dita Kraus, a prisoner at Auschwitz-Birkenau, operates a secret school for the children of families who are imprisoned in the death camp.

Joffo, Joseph. Illus. by Vincent Bailly and translated by Edward Gauvin. *A Bag of Marbles: The Graphic Novel*. 2013. 128 pp. Lerner.

Ages. 12-up. Set in 1941 Paris as the threat of German occupation looms, brothers Maurice and Joseph play one last game of marbles before they are forced to disguise themselves to make the journey to a safe zone. This graphic novel is an adaptation of Joseph Joffo's earlier memoir.

Kacer, Kathy, and Jordana Lebowitz. *To Look a Nazi in the Eye: A Teen's Account of a War Criminal Trial.* **2017. 256 pp. Second Story Press.**

Ages 14-up. Nineteen-year-old Jordana Lebowitz, the granddaughter of Holocaust survivors, relates the trial of Oskar Groening, the man responsible for the death of thousands of Jews during World War II.

Yolen, Jane. *Mapping the Bones.* **2018. 432 pp. Philomel, an imprint of Penguin Random House.**

Ages 14-up. Set in Poland in 1942, this fable is about twins Chaim and Gittel, whose father sends them to safety when he is forced to give up their apartment in the ghetto. They are captured by the Nazis and sent to a labor camp.

29 The Giver

LOIS LOWRY

I'm grateful to you, Jonas, because without you I would never have figured out a way to bring about the change. But your role now is to escape. And my role is to stay.

- 1994 NEWBERY MEDAL
- HOUGHTON MIFFLIN HARCOURT REISSUE 2014
- 256 PAGES
- AGES 10-UP

Set in the future in a dystopian society where all individuals practice Sameness and where everything is colorless and void of emotion, twelve-year-olds are about to receive their assignments, or occupations, from the Council of Elders. Assigned a number at birth, the children in the community are given a name in the Ceremony of One. At twelve, they are lined up by their original numbers and await their fate. Jonas, the main character, is apprehensive about the ceremony and is puzzled when they skip over him and move methodically through the group making assignments until they reach the last number.

Jonas's number is finally called, and he is given his life assignment—Receiver of Memory. When Jonas begins his training with the former Receiver, who is now known as the Giver, he receives pleasant memories—sunsets, sailing, holidays—that existed before Sameness. Eventually he is forced to experience unpleasant emotions—sadness, loneliness, and pain.

His isolation grows as he begins to experience things his family and friends will never experience. Jonas is forced to make a decision that will affect his future when he learns that Gabriel, a baby his family has been tending, is to be "released" for failing to thrive. Before becoming the Receiver, Jonas thought that being "released" meant going to Elsewhere. Now he understands that it means being put to death. To make matters worse, Jonas's father, who is a Nurturer, is assigned to do the release. Before daybreak, Jonas and Gabriel escape, embarking on a dangerous journey to Elsewhere. Their ultimate fate is unknown.

There are three companion novels: *Gathering Blue* (2000), *Messenger* (2004), and *Son* (2012). The graphic novel of *The Giver*, adapted and illustrated by P. Craig Russell, was published to high acclaim in 2019.

BEFORE READING

Tell readers that dystopia means "bad place," and utopia is "an ideal place." Ask them to share a dystopian novel that they have read. An example is *The Hunger Games* by Suzanne Collins. Discuss the popularity of such novels. How does reading about a dystopian society make one think about a more utopian world? Explain how utopia is subjective.

SHARED DISCUSSION

- Describe the community in which Jonas lives. Discuss the advantages and disadvantages of "Sameness." At what point does Jonas understand "Sameness"? How does this understanding contribute to the conflict of the novel?
- "It was one of the rituals, the evening telling of feelings." What other rituals or rules must Jonas follow before the Ceremony of Twelve?
- Jonas remarks that loving another person must have been a dangerous way to live. Describe the relationships between Jonas and his family; his friends Asher and Fiona; and the Giver. Are any

of these relationships dangerous? Perhaps the most dangerous is that between Jonas and the Giver—the one relationship built on love. Why is that relationship dangerous, and what does the danger suggest about the nature of love?

- Explain Jonas's feelings when he learns the meaning of "release."

- Discuss why the Giver shows Jonas the videotape of his father's release of the baby twin. Debate whether the Giver is hoping Jonas will leave the community, thus releasing his memories.

- *The Giver* has been challenged because of the topic of euthanasia. Discuss why the society in which Jonas lives practices euthanasia. How does this practice contribute to Jonas's decision to leave at the end of the novel?

- All adolescents in Jonas's community are given pills when they begin to experience the "stirrings." What is the purpose of the pills? Explain why adult readers are bothered by this practice. How does this practice further define the purpose of the community?

- There have also been concerns expressed because boys bathe old women in the novel. Why is this a nonissue in Jonas's community?

WRITING PROMPTS AND ACTIVITIES

- Jonas never wrote a letter to his family and friends before he ran away. Write a letter that Jonas might have written trying to explain why he left the community.

- Read the biblical story of the archangel Gabriel in the New Testament. Write a journal entry that discusses the significance of the name of the condemned baby in the novel.

- *The Giver* pictures a community in which every person and their experience is precisely the same. Is this loss of diversity worthwhile? Write a journal entry that discusses how our differences make us distinctly human.

- Write a journal entry that discusses the symbolism of the river that borders Jonas's community.
- *The Giver* was challenged soon after it was named the Newbery Medal winner. Write a guest editorial for a newspaper that explains to censors the concept of the novel. Point out how euthanasia and "sexual content" help readers connect to the overall meaning of the book. Cite specific passages from the book to support your thoughts.

READ-ALIKES

Christopher, John. *The White Mountains*. 2014 (reissue). 272 pp. Aladdin, an imprint of Simon & Schuster.

Ages 12-up. Before they turn fourteen and are "capped" by despotic machine creatures called Tripods, Will and his friends undertake a daring escape to a free colony in the White Mountains.

Frankel, Jordana. *The Ward*. 2013. 480 pp. HarperCollins.

Ages 12-up. Set in Manhattan in the near future, sixteen-year-old Renata Dane tries to save her foster sister from a devastating disease caused by pollution. The government hires Renata to find fresh water, but she runs head-on into people consumed by deceit and lies.

Nelson, O. T. Illus. by Jöelle Jones and Jenn Manley Lee and adapted by Dan Jolley. *The Girl Who Owned a City: The Graphic Novel*. 2012. 128 pp. Graphic Universe, an imprint of Lerner.

Ages 10-up. Based on the 1975 novel by the same title, this graphic novel is about a deadly plague that hits the city and kills everyone over the age of twelve, leaving the city to be run by the children. Ten-year-old Lisa emerges as the leader, but the task is almost too much for her.

Shusterman, Neal. *Unwind*. 2007. 352 pp. Simon & Schuster.

Ages 12-up. Living in a futuristic society where the body parts of unwanted teens are harvested, three teens about to become victims of their society run away with the idea of staying on the run until they turn eighteen, when they can't be harmed.

Silver, Shana. *Mind Games.* **2019. 311 pp. Swoon Reads, an imprint of Macmillan.**

Ages 12-up. Arden has the unusual ability to hack into the memories of classmates and upload the experience into someone else's brain as if they had lived it themselves. She has a lucrative business going until the day her own memories are hacked.

The House of the Scorpion

NANCY FARMER

No one can tell the difference between a clone and a human. That's because there isn't any difference. The idea of clones being inferior is a filthy lie.

- 2002 NATIONAL BOOK AWARD FOR YOUNG PEOPLE
- 2003 NEWBERY HONOR BOOK
- 2003 MICHAEL L. PRINTZ HONOR BOOK
- ATHENEUM/RICHARD JACKSON BOOKS, AN IMPRINT OF SIMON & SCHUSTER 2002
- 400 PAGES
- AGES 12–UP

Matt is a clone of El Patrón, a powerful drug lord of the land of Opium, a narrow strip of land between the United States and Mexico. For six years, he has lived in a tiny cottage in the poppy fields with Celia, a kind and deeply religious servant woman who is charged with his care and safety.

He knows little about his existence until he is discovered by a group of children playing in the fields and wonders why he isn't like them. He wants to play and injures himself when he jumps out the window to join their games. He is taken to El Patrón's main house, where his injuries are treated by the drug lord's great-grandson. When he realizes that Matt is a clone, he locks Matt up and treats him like an animal. El Patrón learns what happened to Matt and orders a bodyguard to watch over him and keep him safe. Though Matt has been spared the fate of most other clones, who have their intelligence destroyed at birth, the evil inhabitants of El Patrón's empire consider him a "beast" and an "eejit."

When El Patrón dies at the age of 146, fourteen-year-old Matt escapes Opium with the help of Celia and Tam Lin, his devoted bodyguard, who wants to right his own wrongs. After a near misadventure during his escape, Matt makes his way back home and discovers that the entire population is dead from drinking the poisoned wine that El Patrón had intended to be drunk at his funeral. This means that Matt is now the only heir to the Alacrán legacy. He takes the name El Patrón and begins to rid the country of its evils. *The Lord of Opium* (2013) continues Matt's story.

BEFORE READING

Ask readers to define "science fiction." Then have them discuss the meaning of "cloning." Debate whether a novel about cloning is, according to their definition, considered science fiction.

SHARED DISCUSSION

- Matteo Alacrán is the clone of El Patrón, the lord of the country called Opium, and lives in isolation until children playing in the poppy fields discover him. Why is he so eager to talk to the children, after he is warned against it?

- Describe Matt's relationship with Celia. Why is she the servant chosen to care for Matt? Celia snaps at Matt when he calls her mama. Then she says to him, "I love you more than anything in the world. Never forget that. But you were only loaned to me, *mi vida.*" Why doesn't she explain the term "loaned" to Matt?

- Rosa describes El Patrón as a bandit. How has El Patrón stolen the lives of all those living on his estate? Which characters are his evil partners?

- El Patrón celebrates his 143rd birthday with a large party. Though Matt was "harvested" and doesn't really have a birthday, the celebration is for him as well, since he is El Patrón's clone. How does Matt imitate El Patrón's power when he demands a birthday kiss from María? Discuss how El Patrón encourages Matt's uncharacteristic behavior. Why is María so humiliated by Matt's demand? How does Matt feel the crowd's disapproval?

- What gives Celia the courage to stand up to El Patrón and refuse to let Matt be used for a heart transplant?
- The novel has been challenged because the police and border security essentially run the drug production in the novel. Explain how this helps define the empire that El Patrón has built. Discuss ways to explain to censors the benefits of reading about the evil forces of the country of Opium.
- There are school officials who are uncomfortable with the novel being taught because of its portrayal of cloning. How do these officials focus on a topic rather than the underlying meaning of the entire book? What would you want them to know about the novel and Matt's journey at the end?
- The novel has been challenged because it was deemed "unsuitable" for the age group. For what age do you think the book is suitable?

WRITING PROMPTS AND ACTIVITIES

- After the children discover Matt, he is taken from Celia and imprisoned in a stall for six months with only straw for a bed. Write an essay that discusses how prison is a metaphor for his entire life. Who is the warden of the prison? Include a concluding paragraph that discusses how María, Celia, and Tam Lin help him escape prison.
- Write an essay that explains what El Patrón means when he says to Celia, "We make a fine pair of scorpions, don't we." Explain why she is insulted by this comment.
- Considering that Matt is the clone of El Patrón, have the class

sponsor a debate that argues whether environment influences evil more than genetics.

- Dolly, the first mammal to be successfully cloned from an adult cell, was born on July 5, 1996, at the Roslin Institute in Edinburgh, Scotland. The sheep died by lethal injection in 2003 at age six. Use books in the library or sites on the internet to locate more information about Dolly, and then write a brief journal entry about the significance of her birth to science.

- Write a brief journal entry that discusses Esperanza's role in helping Matt gain his ultimate freedom life as a human.

READ-ALIKES

Cave, Patrick. *Sharp North*. 2009. 528 pp. Simon & Schuster.

Ages 14-up. This futuristic novel is set in Great Britain, where clones are called "spares." Mira, the main character, is on a mission to discover who and what she is.

Gaither, Stefanie. *Falls the Shadow*. 2015. 352 pp. Simon & Schuster.

Ages 12-up. When twelve-year-old Cate's sister, Violet, dies, her parents clone her. Then the daughter of an anti-cloner is murdered, and it is believed that Violet is responsible for the crime. *Into the Abyss* (2016) is the sequel.

Hautman, Pete. *Rash*. 2007. 272 pp. Simon & Schuster.

Ages 14-up. Set in 2074, teenager Bo Marsten knows that his country has made rules to make it "safe," but when he causes trouble because of a bad temper, he is sentenced to factory labor in the Canadian tundra.

Koosis, Lisa A. *Resurrecting Sunshine*. 2016. 320 pp. Albert Whitman.

Ages 14-up. It's the year 2036, and Adam is mourning the death of his girlfriend, Sunshine, when the authorities from Project Orpheus ask for his help in cloning her.

Patrick, Cat. *The Originals*. 2013. 304 pp. Little, Brown.

Ages 14-up. Three seventeen-year-old sisters share one life because their mother, a genetics scientist, cloned them using her own eggs.

TEACHER'S AND BOOK DISCUSSION GUIDE

A complete Teacher's and Discussion Guide is available on the publisher's website.

PART VI

THIS WAS MY LIFE

Memoirs provide readers with a glimpse into one aspect of an author's life. They are often about resilience, hope, and the ultimate journey to success. Those who read memoirs gain insight and inspiration into personal struggles, and they find joy in the celebration of the writer's accomplishments. Sometimes these memoirs reveal "tough" beginnings in families that don't have the capacity to be supportive. Other writers have excellent support from extended family but cannot function in the rudimentary system of the nation's schools and colleges. For some it takes a while to find their place in the world. The young should be exposed to memoirs so that they understand the strength and toughness it takes to realize one's potential and fulfill their dreams.

31 Bad Boy: A Memoir

WALTER DEAN MYERS

I was sixteen and adrift. I had no ideas, no plans, and little hope.

- HARPERCOLLINS 2001
- 224 PAGES
- AGES 12-UP

Walter Dean Myers was born in West Virginia, but when he was two, he was given to Florence (the first wife of his biological father) and Herbert Dean, who lived in New York's Harlem. Myers was loved by his adoptive parents, and he remembers his mother reading to him. He was a very bright boy but didn't do well in school. Born with a speech impediment, he was reluctant to speak up in class at the risk of being laughed at by the other students. At PS 125 on Lasalle Street, he was labeled a "bad boy" and spent a lot of time in isolation or in the principal's office. His mother didn't know what to do about his behavior except to beat him, which was a common practice in those days. Myers makes it clear that while this may be considered abuse today, it wasn't then.

Myers felt like he was part of his neighborhood, playing stick ball in the streets and basketball in a nearby park. He was taller and bigger than most of his friends, which made him a perfect candidate for becoming an outstanding athlete. This wasn't the path he took. Instead he turned to reading, and he devoured every book that was suggested to him. Finally, a male sixth-grade teacher, who recognized the boy's ability, went home with him one day to have a talk with Florence Dean about her son. This was a turning point for Myers because it was the first time a teacher had actually shown interest in his well-being.

At the end of his sixth-grade year, Myers took a test to enter a rapid advancement class. He was accepted and completed the seventh-and eighth-grade curriculum in one year. In ninth grade, he entered Stuyvesant High School, which took him out of his neighborhood and into a school with high-achieving students with more diverse backgrounds. Stuyvesant opened his eyes to racism. He could attend classes with white students, but he wasn't invited to their parties because he was Black. He began skipping school and finally dropped out altogether during his senior year. The Vietnam War had begun, and Myers joined the army on his seventeenth birthday.

Inspired by the works of James Baldwin, Myers gained courage to write about growing up in Harlem and about his own troubled childhood. He remembered the teachers who recognized his writing ability, and he never stopped reading and writing. He died in 2014, having written more than one hundred books. He was the third U.S. National Ambassador for Young People's Literature.

BEFORE READING

Ask readers to consider the title of this memoir and discuss what they think is the overall theme of the book. Why is it important for young readers to know the journeys of people who have beaten all odds and realized their dreams?

SHARED DISCUSSION

- Describe Walter's family. How was his relationship with his mother different from his relationship with his father? Explain how his father changed after Uncle Lee was killed. What eventually pulled his father out of his sadness?

- Walter Dean Myers discovered books and reading at a very young age. Discuss why he kept this passion to himself.

- Describe Walter's teachers. Why did Mrs. Parker, his fourth-grade teacher, think that he was a bully? Mrs. Conway labeled him a "bad boy." How did his relationship with Mrs. Conway change after she led him to books? Discuss how Mr. Lasher related to Myers. Debate whether this was a turning point for him.

- Myers had a tough time in class. What does he mean when he says he had a need to "feel the spaces"? Discuss how writing filled those spaces when he became an adult.

- At what point in his life did Myers become aware of racism? How did he deal with it? Explain how the racism he endured shaped his writing.

- Mrs. Dodson, a woman whom Myers called the Wicked Witch of West Harlem, claimed that comic books were a "road map to the jailhouse." Explain how this is an attitude of a censor. Consider the popularity of graphic novels today. How would you defend reading comic books and graphic novels to a woman like Mrs. Dodson?

- This memoir has been challenged because of "gang violence" and "drug use." Discuss how violence and drug use were very much a part of Myers's neighborhood. How could Myers have written a memoir that didn't include this very real part of his childhood?

- Parents have complained about the books because Myers questions religion. Church was very much a part of Myers's youth. At what point did he begin to question religion? Myers wrote a letter to Reverend Robinson that expressed his doubts about God. Explain the response that Myers received from the minister. Discuss why some people are troubled by this part of Myers's memoir. How do people have different religious journeys? Debate how recognizing these differences is important in our current society.

WRITING PROMPTS AND ACTIVITIES

- A memoir should have a very distinct theme. Write a short journal entry that explains the central theme of Myers's memoir. Cite specific passages and use direct quotes to support your thoughts.
- In *Bad Boy: A Memoir*, Walter Dean Myers says, "My life was filled with the cultural substance of blackness." Read at least one novel by Myers, and write a journal entry that shows how his culture and community influenced his writing.
- Walter Dean Myers wrote a poem titled "My Mother" that his elementary school published. Consider his relationship with his mother, and write a poem titled "His Mother."
- A good memoir is written from the heart. Write a brief journal entry that discusses the "heart" in *Bad Boy: A Memoir*. Cite specific passages, and use direct quotes to support your thoughts.
- Walter Dean Myers loved comic books. Select an action-filled part from his memoir and create a six-panel comic strip that communicates the scene.

READ-ALIKES

Crutcher, Chris. *King of the Mild Frontier: An Ill-Advised Autobiography*. 2004. 272 pp. Greenwillow, an imprint of HarperCollins.

Ages 12-up. Crutcher shares his own adolescent struggles with his parents, his bad temper, and his journey to becoming a family therapist and successful writer of young adult books.

Noah, Trevor. *It's Trevor Noah: Born a Crime*. 2019. 304 pp. Delacorte, an imprint of Penguin Random House.

Ages 10-up. In this memoir, Noah, a host on Comedy Central's *The*

Daily Show, reveals what it was like growing up a biracial child in South Africa, where racism affected choices he made, and how he gained success against all odds.

Paulsen, Gary. *The Beet Fields: Memories of a Sixteenth Summer*. **2011. 176 pp. Delacorte, an imprint of Penguin Random House.**

Ages 12-up. This autobiographical novel relates the story of one boy's difficult journey from runaway to carnival worker and what it was like dealing with immense sadness and loneliness until one day he found a true purpose.

Pitts, Byron. *Be the One: Six True Stories of Teens Overcoming Hardship with Hope*. **2017. 128 pp. Simon & Schuster.**

Ages 12-up. The author interviews six self-determined teens who managed to survive lives of abandonment, abuse, bullying, drug addiction, mental illness, violence, extreme poverty, and the quest to find their purpose in life.

Wolff, Tobias. *This Boy's Life: A Memoir*. **2000. 304 pp. Grove/Atlantic.**

Ages 14-up. Though he wrote his memoir for adults, Wolff, a successful writer and college professor, relates his "bad boy" adolescence, which includes running away and stealing cars, and what it was like living in a house with a loving mother and a hostile stepfather.

32 Hole in My Life

JACK GANTOS

I had a strong sense that I needed to snap off my past in order to have a future.

- MICHAEL L. PRINTZ HONOR 2003
- FARRAR, STRAUS & GIROUX, AN
  IMPRINT OF MACMILLAN 2002
- 208 PAGES
- AGES 12-UP

Jack Gantos, writer of award-winning books for children and young adults, tells the story of his tumultuous teen years and his path to becoming a writer. Things weren't always good at home, and when Gantos was still in high school, his father, always looking for a get-rich-quick job, moves his family to St. Croix in the U.S. Virgin Islands. Jack remains behind to finish high school in Fort Lauderdale. He lives in a boardinghouse until he is kicked out for drinking. Homeless with barely enough money to survive, he lands a job at Piggly Wiggly and moves into Kings Court, a run-down motel, where he finds himself in the middle of the juvenile marijuana scene. He finally drops out of high school and joins his family in St. Croix.

Racial tensions are high on the island, and finding a decent job is almost impossible until he makes a deal with Rik, a drug smuggler. He offers Jack $1,000 to help him smuggle drugs to New York. Believing the money could get him into college and on his way to realizing his dream of being a writer, Jack sets sail with Rik's associate. Along the way, Jack keeps a journal that details his concerns and fears about his part in this criminal venture.

When their boat docks in New York, Jack is arrested and sentenced for up to six years in the low-security Federal Correctional Institution in Ashland, Kentucky. By day, he works as an X-ray technician and medical assistant, and by night he sits alone in his cell and writes about the horrors of prison life in the margins of *The Brothers Karamazov,* a book he borrowed from the prison library. Jack concentrates on good behavior and makes a plan to attend school, which helps get him a shorter prison term. On the day he checks out of prison, the guards force him to leave behind the book that holds his own words about prison life, but he eagerly enters school and draws on his experiences to find his voice and write meaningful and entertaining fiction.

BEFORE READING

Jack Gantos believed that he needed adventure before he could write. In his case, the adventure turned dark. Ask readers to write a journal entry that describes in great detail a particular adventure that they have experienced. What did they learn from the adventure? Ask for volunteers to read their writing.

SHARED DISCUSSION

- Describe Jack's family. Why do Jack's parents allow him to remain in Florida when they move to St. Croix? How is this decision the beginning of Jack's troubles?
- Discuss the bad decisions that Gantos make in his youth. At what point does he begin making good decisions? Explain how he learns from his mistakes.
- How does Jack's prison job as an X-ray technician and medical assistant give him a broader view of prison life? Discuss the violence at the Ashland prison. How does witnessing these acts of violence make Jack realize that he needs a goal so that he may get out of prison early?

- Describe Jack's journey from St. Croix to the Northeast. Discuss how Hamilton, Rik's assistant, treats him. How is Jack naïve about this sea journey? Debate whether he should have asked more questions before embarking on the journey.

- Throughout his tough life experiences, Jack continues to read. How does his love of literature take him to Key West? Explain how *The Brothers Karamazov* influences him when he is in prison. Why don't the prison guards allow him to take the book with him when he leaves prison?

- Gantos's memoir has been challenged because of the drug culture depicted in it. What might readers learn from Gantos about the dangers and consequences of drug smuggling?

- Violence at the prison in Ashland is another reason that the book has been challenged. Explain why it's important to know about such prison violence. How might Gantos's memoir spark good conversation about prison life and reform?

- Some people have challenged the books because they feel it's not age-appropriate. The memoir is written for young adults, which means the targeted age is twelve and up. How would you explain to a school or library board that this is the appropriate age?

WRITING PROMPTS AND ACTIVITIES

- A memoir is one aspect of a writer's life, and it has a continuous theme. An autobiography is a chronological account of a person's life. Write a journal entry that explains why *Hole in My Life* is a memoir. Discuss the continuous theme, using direct quotes and scenes from the book to support your thoughts.

- Gantos says, "I wanted books to change me, and I wanted to write books that would change others." Write a journal entry that discusses how *Hole in My Life* could change readers.

- When Jack docks in New York, he takes some of the hash and buries it in Central Park. Write a journal entry that explains why Jack never goes back for it.
- Jack Gantos has commented "Someone once said anyone can be great under rosy circumstances, but the true test of character is measured by how well a person makes decisions during difficult times." Select one of the difficult times that Gantos writes about and write an essay about the decisions he made and how they shaped his writing.
- Write a one-page essay that discusses why the *Karamazov* journal is such a great loss for Gantos.

READ-ALIKES

Gantos, Jack. *Jack's Black Book*. 1999. 176 pp. Square Fish, an imprint of Macmillan.

Ages 10–14. This semiautobiographical novel, the last in the Jack Henry series, is funny and sometimes dark as Jack Henry records his terrible circumstances in a black book.

Gantos, Jack. *The Trouble in Me*. 2017. 240 pp. Square Fish, an imprint of Macmillan.

Ages 12-up. This autobiography reveals how Gantos, a follower, emulated a neighbor who had just returned from juvenile detention. His behaviors landed him in prison as well.

Gantos, Jack. *Writing Radar: Using Your Journal to Snoop Out and Craft Great Stories*. 2019. 224 pp. Square Fish, an imprint of Macmillan.

Ages 10-up. Using passages from his books to illustrate how ideas develop to form a story, Gantos offers young writers tips on how to journal and turn their writing into longer narratives.

Paulsen, Gary. *Guts: The True Stories Behind Hatchet and the Brian Books.* **2002. 260 pp. Laurel Leaf, an imprint of Penguin Random House.**

Ages 10–14. The son of alcoholic parents, Paulsen had a tumultuous childhood, and was forced to learn survival skills, which he transformed into ideas for his main character in the Brian books.

Small, David. *Stitches: A Memoir.* **2009. 320 pp. W. W. Norton.**

Ages 14-up. This graphic memoir depicts Small's deeply troubled childhood and his journey to follow his dreams and become an artist.

ABOUT THE AUTHOR

Pat R. Scales is a retired middle and high school librarian in Greenville, SC. She has also served as adjunct instructor of children's and young adult literature at Furman University and has been a guest lecturer at universities across the nation. A First Amendment advocate, she is a former chair of American Library Association's Intellectual Freedom Committee and serves on the Board of Advisors of the National Coalition Against Censorship and is a member of the Freedom to Read Foundation. She is a past president of the Association of Library Service to Children and in 2011 received the Distinguished Service Award. She chaired the 1992 Newbery Award Committee, the 2003 Caldecott Award Committee, and the 2001 Laura Ingalls Wilder Award Committee. She writes a bimonthly column "Scales on Censorship" for *School Library Journal.* She is the author of *Teaching Banned Books: 12 Guides for Young Readers; Protecting Intellectual Freedom in Your School Library; Books Under Fire: A Hit List of Banned and Challenged Children's Books; Defending Frequently Challenged Young Adult Books;* and *Encourage Reading from the Start.*

ABOUT THE AMERICAN LIBRARY ASSOCIATION

The American Library Association (ALA) is the foremost national organization providing resources to inspire library and information professionals to transform their communities through essential programs and services. ALA condemns censorship and works to ensure free access to information. Every year, ALA's Office for Intellectual Freedom (OIF) compiles a list of the Top 10 Most Challenged Books in order to inform the public about censorship in libraries and schools. The lists are based on information from media stories and voluntary reports sent to OIF from communities across the U.S.

Learn more about how you can stay connected to what's going on in libraries and how you can help advocate for your own library at ilovelibraries.org.